Licensing

Selfishness

Other Books by Paul Brownback

The Danger of Self-Love: Re-Examining a Popular Myth

How to Succeed as CEO of Your Life: 12 Spiritual Principles I Wish I Had Learned Long Ago

This is the Generation: Proof from Scripture that Christ Will Return in This Generation

LICENSING

SELFISHNESS

THE SECULAR AND EVANGELICAL IDEOLOGY DESTROYING AMERICA

Paul Brownback, PhD

Foundation Stone Press

Dedication

To my parents
Lloyd and Helen Brownback
Who lived for others

Table of Contents

SECTION ONE PROMOTING SELFISHNESS 1

Chapter 1: When Good People Are Weak 5

Chapter 2: Why Licensing Selfishness Is Deadly 21

SECTION TWO IDEOLOGY OF SELFISHNESS 41

Chapter 1: Paving the Way for Our Current Culture 43

Chapter 2: Cultural Invasion 53

Chapter 3: Agape-Destroying Culture 65

SECTION THREE   PSYCHOLOGY OF SELFISHNESS 83

Chapter 1: The Psychological Theory Shaping American Culture 85

Chapter 2: The Experiment 97

Chapter 3: Societal Destruction 109

SECTION FOUR   EVANGELICAL INFILTRATION AND THE IMPACT 123

Chapter 1: Evangelical Infiltration and Its New 125

Belief System 125

Chapter 2: Does God Love and Accept Unconditionally? 145

Chapter 3: Selfishness and Agape Production 167

Chapter 4: Damages Inflicted by Unconditional 175

Acceptance 175

SECTION FIVE RECOVERING AND WINNING 185

Chapter 1: Road to Recovery 187

Chapter 2: Winning 201

Acknowledgments

I would like to thank my dear wife, Connie, for giving good recommendations and proofing yet another book and for her willingness to live a widow's existence during the many hours I worked on it.

I also want to express special thanks to Don Otis, Publicist and President of Veritas Communications, for not only providing significant help but also extending remarkable patience and kindness.

SECTION ONE
PROMOTING SELFISHNESS

It's worse than you think.

This book deals with something far beyond our human inclination toward selfishness. That is an old story started in the Garden of Eden that will only end when we step through the gates of heaven. I struggle with selfishness daily and lose the fight too often. I am betting that you experience the same. That is bad enough.

However, the current proliferation of selfishness does not merely result from normal cultural erosion. It is licensed by an ideology of selfishness, an interconnected ideology, psychology, and theology that unleashes selfishness in both secular society and the evangelical church. Selfishness comprises a powerful human inclination without any encouragement. An ideology that protects and even promotes selfishness has put it on steroids, creating societal chaos.

Even worse, this ideology has become the predominant element of contemporary American culture, driving our values and morals. Consequently, selfishness underlies virtually every problem confronting America today. The current riots manifest a gross display of selfishness, wrecking homes and businesses of others to vent frustration or make a political point. The selfish inclination of many politicians to make decisions for their own benefit rather than for those they represent is inflicting untold harm on our nation. The mainstream media consistently misrepresenting events to advance their political agenda also provides us with a malevolent manifestation of selfishness. One is hard-pressed to identify any contemporary societal problem that does not have selfishness at its root.

But it gets worse. Normal selfishness, seeking to benefit self at the expense of another, is bad enough. This ideology legitimizes selfishness by denying personhood to all others—by reducing them to objects in one's field of experience. This leaves no other real person to infringe on the right of the individual to live selfishly. He is free to behave as he pleases. He is god in his own universe.

This display of sovereign selfishness shows itself in abortion. My denial of the personhood of an innocent child licenses me to take his life.

An article by Matt Walsh entitled "The Confused and Pointless Rage Of An Entitled Generation," discusses Julie Clark, an activist who decided to close some streets to protest siren/noise pollution. She Tweeted, "As we blocked off streets we demanded that people turn around. This was a minor inconvenience for this affluent white neighborhood." Julie became incensed when a driver refused to observe her blockade. In reflecting on her attitude, Walsh observes, "She doesn't seem to realize, or care, that other humans actually exist on the planet, and that just because she feels like it would be fun and worthwhile to shut down part of the city, that arrangement may not work for everyone else."[1] Here Julie Clark views herself as the only real person, therefore possessing a license to do whatever she pleases and becoming indignant when the rest of the world does not cooperate.

David Horowitz records a more destructive example of this attitude in his book *Blitz: Trump Will Smash the Left and Win*. He reflects on a statement by Sen. Kamala Harris, who during a

Democrat presidential primary debate addresses Pres. Trump through the television with this message:

> Pres. Trump, you spent the last two and a half years full-time trying to sell hate and division among us. You have used hate, intimidation, fear, and over 12,000 lies as a way to distract from your failed policies and your broken promises.[2]

This was not a statement of political disagreement but an attempt to destroy a human being using false accusations. Horowitz goes on to demonstrate that none of these accusations are true. Not to worry. Just as the person opting for an abortion assumes the right to kill an unborn baby, our ideology of selfishness licensed Harris to assassinate the character of the President.

But it gets worse than that. This ideology of selfishness has now infiltrated the evangelical belief system. Evangelicals have embraced it as a core concept, governing their relationship with God and their approach to life. Consequently, the church, God's means of rescuing society from selfishness, is not only failing to do so but embracing and disseminating the very ideology that is destroying secular society. Because God assigned to the church the roles of salt and light, this situation is resulting not only in the spiritual decline of evangelical Christianity but the demise of America.

If this trend is not reversed, our nation is headed for certain destruction. Only the evangelical church can provide a solution. Politics can play an important subsidiary role, but ultimately we cannot expect secular society to rescue us from selfishness. Only the church, possessing the power of the Holy Spirit can achieve that. However, the church can only achieve that objective if it recognizes that it is licensing selfishness and adopts the biblical alternative. The objectives of this book are to identify this ideology that is licensing selfishness in secular society and the church, to expose its destructive nature, and to reveal the biblical alternative.

Chapter 1: When Good People Are Weak

The Minority Dominating the Majority

How might we characterize Europe's response to Muslim immigrants? An unflattering but accurate descriptive term might be—*groveling*. A relatively small Muslim minority dominates and imposes its will on the European majority.

Examples abound of this embarrassment. Though Britain has at least summoned enough strength to extricate itself from the European Union, it nonetheless reflects the European penchant for weakness. A flagrant demonstration resides in the grooming and rape by Muslim men of thousands of British girls, many of them underage. Most pathetic is the unwillingness of the British to do anything substantive to deal with this evil, though they are well aware of the situation. What could be more craven than cowering before a group of minority men who are raping your underage daughters? Majorities in Sweden, Germany, and other European nations are displaying similar spinelessness.

This state of affairs is especially pathetic considering that these countries belong to the Europeans. They have ruled them for centuries. Muslims for the most part are newcomers and cultural outsiders. They have no basis for insisting on their way, for imposing their culture. In addition, the Europeans control the government, the military, the police force, and the purse strings.

Yet the Europeans cower before them. Why? Because Europeans have become weakened by socialism. Lara Logan, in her article, "France: Less Work, More Time Off," exposes the weakness with which socialism infects the European character.

> "There are millions of people...who take endless vacations in the summer—a month, two months, even more. We're not talking about the idle rich. These are government employees, blue-collar workers, office clerks. How do they manage this? What's their secret?
>
> They live in France...."3

Full-time workers in France are guaranteed five weeks of vacation, have a maximum workweek of 35 hours, and enjoy dozens of public holidays. Socialistic leisure has weakened the European character, leaving them too sick to ward off Muslim domination.

Instead, weakened by socialism, Europeans grovel, hoping that Muslim immigrants will replace their own children, whom they have aborted, in order to maintain an economy that will support their pension funds in their old age, which is wishful thinking at best.

History abounds with examples of smaller but culturally stronger populations that have subdued weak majorities. Perhaps this development works for the best when the weak majority culture is overrun by a minority that is more moral and energetic. It is counterproductive, however, when the dominating minority advances destructive beliefs. Think for example of the dominance of Germany by a Nazi minority or czarist Russia overrun by a minority

of communists. It is true that the majorities in these nations displayed sickness that
required a cure, but they were overpowered by minorities with destructive agendas that ultimately cost millions of lives.

These examples reveal that any culture with a strong belief system possesses the power to defeat those with a weaker one. However, these examples also demonstrate that a strong belief system is not necessarily a good one, does not necessarily possess the potential to produce a healthy and successful culture. Though communism possessed the power to dominate czarist Russia, it did not have the capability to transform Russia into a healthy and successful nation. It was likewise with Nazi Germany. Consequently, it is of vital importance that good cultures remain strong.

The American Phenomenon

This book asserts that a similar process is occurring in America, with a culturally stronger minority dominating a weak majority. That majority consists of those Americans committed to traditional American values, the belief system that made America a great nation. Progressives comprise the aggressive minority that has been seizing control over our nation beginning with the 1960s. It now dominates the mainstream news media, the entertainment media, social media, the Democrat Party, our public schools and universities, the deep state, and other significant elements of our society.

We must distinguish between progressives and liberals. Both make their home primarily in the Democrat Party. Both reject Christianity, or at least any form of Christianity remotely reflecting the biblical version. Consequently, both advance a litany of unbiblical causes such as abortion and the LGBTQ agenda. Both advocate big government as the means of promoting their initiatives. However, more traditional liberals pursued their objectives using reasoned arguments and the political process. Progressives overtly reject facts and reason, replacing them with raw power, imposing their will through anarchy and shutting down free speech.

Progressive Dominance

Progressives have for some time been the dominant force in our universities, producing graduates in journalism, teaching, government, and a wide variety of other fields. These graduates have now gained positions of power and are using them to propagate progressive causes. They have now taken control of the Democrat party. They also exercise vast power by occupying prominent positions in the mainstream media. The CEOs and boards of major corporations flood progressive causes with substantial financial support. Therefore, though these progressives represent a minority of Americans, by seizing positions of power they are succeeding in the domination of our society.

This domination shows itself in the 1962 and 1963 Supreme Court decisions to ban prayer and Bible reading from public schools, the 1973 Roe V Wade decision legalizing abortion, and the 2015 decision legalizing gay marriage. Progressive advances also manifest themselves in American culture as evidence by the propagation of their values through the entertainment industry and by many other means.

Perhaps the most crushing display of progressive domination resides in its eradication of freedom of speech. Progressives may freely express their ideas publicly while conservatives are muted. In most places of employment, a person can speak freely in favor of homosexuality, transgender issues, women's rights, etc., but the person expressing conservative views exposes himself to the prospects of censure or dismissal.

This speech suppression manifested itself in the firing of longtime shock jock and Sacramento Kings TV play-by-play announcer Grant Napear. It only took three words to destroy his long and illustrious career. He tweeted, "All lives matter."[4] Some on the left viewed this expression as a putdown of the Black Lives Matter movement, which led to his firing. The totalitarian nature of this development shows itself in the slightness of the offense, if any existed at all. The phrase, "All lives matter" comprises an expression of goodness, Napear insisted that he did not intend to demean

"Black lives matter," and his long career has been untarnished by racism. The fact that someone viewed these three words as racist was enough to destroy him.

David Harsanyi, writing in National Review, observes:

> We're in the dawn of a high-tech, bloodless Cultural Revolution; one that relies on intimidation, public shaming, and economic ruin to dictate what words and ideas are permissible in the public square.
>
> "Words are violence" has always been an illiberal notion meant to stifle speech and open discourse. Popularized by a generation of coddled and brittle college students, it now guides policy on editorial pages at newspapers such as the Philadelphia Inquirer, the New York Times, and most major news outlets.[5]

This control of speech demonstrates the progressive domination over American society. It also secures that domination by preventing conservatives from expressing opposition. This speech control is essential to the progressive movement because their positions are not undergirded either by fact or reason, and therefore they must protect themselves from rational exposure by muting opponents. Their capacity to do so is allowing them to relentlessly advance their agenda. Unless something changes, unless they are stopped, their domination will soon be complete and irreversible.

Andrew Klavan says this about the relentless progressive advance:

> One of the great disadvantages of having ceded the culture to the Left is that conservatives are always on defense. Because the Left owns the news media, the entertainment media, and the academy – the Empire of Lies, as I call it – they set the agenda, and all we can do is fight back. We think we're winning when we repulse their attacks, but you can't win on defense. They will keep coming back again and again until the day is theirs, even if it takes half a century.[6]

Think about the state of America in 1960. It is almost incredible that just six decades ago American children were opening their school day with Bible reading and prayer, that abortion was not legal, that recreational drugs were virtually unheard of, and that almost everyone assumed that marriage entailed a relationship between a man and a woman. The moral deterioration of our society since then exposes the ongoing advance of the progressive agenda.

We might seek comfort in the efforts of Pres. Trump to reverse some progressive gains. However, during his watch the transgender movement has taken significant strides forward, crushing yet another of our moral foundations. Even during a Republican presidency, Progressives continued to progress.

The next section of this book reveals that the progressive agenda is rooted in an ideology that gives license to selfishness. It promotes selfish living as a way of life and even as a moral imperative. It is producing an outpouring of selfishness that is inflicting incalculable harm on America.

Conservative Weakness

The capacity of progressives to impose their agenda leads us to ask the cause of the weakness of the American majority. Traditionally, biblical Christianity energized the American conservative position. Now, many American conservatives lack any serious Christian commitment. They maintain a sentimental attachment to their Christian heritage but no substantive commitment to Christ. Consequently, this conservative segment does not possess the strength to engage in a culture war.

While other conservatives have largely abandoned their Christian commitment, evangelicals have not. They have maintained a substantive commitment to Christ. While other conservatives take on the role of civilians during wartime, evangelicals possess the potential to serve as the army, the only force with the resources for fighting.

This book contends, however, that in their current condition, evangelicals are too weak to engage progressives effectively in the culture war. The weakened condition of evangelicals is particularly devastating because they comprise the only hope for rescuing America from the disastrous agenda of progressives.

Some might view this concern regarding impending defeat as a lack of faith. They comfort themselves in the assurance that God is in control. To this I respond that God was in control when Israel was overrun by Babylon and the men were killed, women raped, and children carried into slavery. God was also in control when Hitler took over Germany, which led to the destruction of that nation and 6 million Jews.

The question is not whether God is in control. He is. The question is whether His people in their current condition provide a conduit through which the Holy Spirit is free to do His work of salvaging our culture. The current inability of evangelicals to prevent the advance of progressive corruption reveals a blockage of the ministry of the Holy Spirit. This book identifies that blockage and offers a biblical alternative.

Viewing the evangelical church as America's only hope makes sense when we recognize that our Christian heritage made America great in the first place. Some conservatives seek to credit America's greatness to factors such as our liberty or our Constitution. Those entities, however, were merely byproducts of our Christian culture. Ultimately it was the influence of God's people establishing a Christian culture that made America great the first time. That being the case, it is only God's people reinstituting a Christian culture that can make America great again.

Resources to Win

Some might contend that evangelicals are losing the culture war because they lack the potential to win. Progressives are just too powerful, supported by the mainstream media, much of the judiciary, the deep state, and other forces.

However, evangelicals possess more than adequate potential to win a culture war. Consider this array of resources at their disposal.

Spiritual Resources

God has given His people the Holy Spirit. Think about what that means. The God of the universe lives within us. Colossians 1:11 says literally that we are "empowered with all power," the word *power* being used twice, once in the verb form and once in the noun form. God provides this power to those committed to Christ and the truth of His Word. In the United States, this contingent includes evangelicals, charismatics, a remnant of believers in liberal churches, conservative Catholics, and others. Throughout this book, I use evangelical as a comprehensive term to refer to those in all these categories.

The power of the Holy Spirit not only provides evangelicals with the potential to transform lives but also to revolutionize culture. It overpowered the Roman Empire, the greatest earthly force of its time, and ultimately shaped Western civilization. David Bentley Hart in his book *Atheist Delusions: The Christian Revolution and Its Fashionable Enemies*, describes the vastness of this achievement:

> ... Among all the many great transitions that have marked the evolution of Western civilization, whether convulsive or gradual, political or philosophical, social or scientific, material or spiritual, there has been only one— the triumph of Christianity—that can be called in the full sense a "revolution": a truly massive and ethical revision of humanity's prevailing vision of reality, so pervasive in its influence and so vast in its consequences as actually to have created a new conception of the world, of history, of human nature, of time, and of the moral good. To my mind, I should add, it was an event immeasurably more impressive in its cultural creativity and more ennobling in its moral power than any other movement of spirit, will, imagination, aspiration, or accomplishment in the history of the West.[7]

The Holy Spirit can likewise empower evangelicals to transform America today.

We also have access to the power of Scripture. When Luther unleashed the Word of God in Germany and Tyndale in England, it transformed those societies.

In addition, both Scripture and history reveal that prayer releases the power of God. The power of prayer spawned many society-transforming revivals and awakenings.

Jesus used the terms salt and light to describe the church's capacities to influence society.

Salt permeates substances and prevents decay. God empowers the church to similarly influence culture. Christian parents, teachers, judges, businessmen, politicians, journalists, and especially homemakers—believers in every walk of life— can promote morality, responsibility, and other Christian virtues.

Preservation requires only a small proportion of salt. A U. S. Department of Agriculture publication reports: "Fortunately the growth of many undesirable organisms normally found in cured meat and poultry products is inhibited at relatively low concentrations of salt."[8] Likewise, a small minority of Christians can inhibit moral decay. Germs exist in every human body but are kept under control in the healthy person. Likewise, all societies manifest some level of corruption. Nonetheless, the church exercising its salt capability can prevent unbridled immorality and produce an essentially just and moral society.

The church functions as light by disseminating truth, that is, a Christian worldview that contains information essential to societal well-being. This light includes the gospel message, which embodies the truth to transform lives. God's truth also informs us regarding spiritual realities, human nature, and how to live effectively in a fallen world. The human eye can see the light of a candle at 1.6 miles.[9] Likewise, a minority of Christians can illumine society with the light of Scripture.

The church exercising its capacities as salt and light will never bring heaven on earth. However, it can maintain a moral and enlightened culture that engenders individual and societal health.

Numeric resources

Evangelicals comprise a significant segment of the population: Though our nation is becoming increasingly secular, a 2019 poll revealed that 65% of Americans still identify as Christian.[10] Between 23% and 24% of Americans affiliate with an evangelical church or denomination.[11] About 34% speak of having a "born-again" experience.[12] Those seriously committed to evangelical doctrine and a biblical lifestyle comprise around 8%.[13]

These statistics indicate that evangelicals possess the potential to mobilize a significant segment of the American population to engage in a culture war.

This evangelical population includes a vast storehouse of human capital. The evangelical church has trained pastors, teachers, and those skilled in supporting fields such as radio, television, the Internet, and education.

A Unifying Belief System

Just as progressives are joined together by their ideology, evangelicals possess a core belief system that can unite and motivate them to engage in the culture war. Though evangelicals have been fragmented over marginal issues, for the most part they agree on central biblical themes such as those expressed in the Apostles Creed. That belief system plus the ministry of the Holy Spirit that binds us together as brothers and sisters provide a foundation for energizing evangelicals in a common cultural cause.

Collateral Resource

In addition, the evangelical church in America possesses a great storehouse of collateral resources, which contribute to its potential to transform society. These capacities surpass those enjoyed by any church in all of history. They include billions of dollars' worth of real estate, many colleges and seminaries, publishing houses, recreational facilities, radio and television studios, and many other types of facilities.

Freedom

Despite current erosions of our freedoms, American Christians still possess significant latitude to function as salt and light.

This vast storehouse of resources and the freedom to employ them arm American evangelicals with the potential for enormous influence. Of all Christians on earth, American believers are best situated to succeed in their roles as salt and light. However, the evangelical church must possess sufficient health to utilize these weapons in the culture war. Currently they do not.

Evangelical Sickness

The demise of liberal mainline denominations during the previous century reveals the necessity of the church maintaining spiritual health. They became infected by the form of liberalism infecting secular culture during that era, resulting in doctrinal corruption and spiritual sickness. At one time these mainline denominations possessed vast numbers, resources, and influence. However, infection by liberal ideas left them sick and dying. This spiritual malaise prevented them from employing their vast resources to maintain a Christian culture in America.

Likewise today, the infiltration of the current secular ideology into the evangelical belief system has left evangelicals too spiritually weak to employ their vast resources listed above to engage effectively in the culture war. In fact, it is preventing the evangelical church per se, denominations and independent churches, actual bodies of believers, from engaging in the war at all.

Three factors expose this AWOL status of the contemporary evangelical church. First, one can go to almost any evangelical church on any given Sunday morning and come away with the impression that the culture war does not exist. Even though innocent babies might be aborted within blocks of the church, even though many students from church families might be attending schools that are indoctrinating them with a destructive worldview, even though the left is curtailing freedoms of businesspeople attending the church, prayers are made and sermons delivered without any hint that an enemy force is seeking our destruction and making substantial progress in that direction.

This almost total disregard for our present danger leads to a second indicator of the evangelical church's AWOL status. Evangelical churches and denominations have delegated their responsibilities to engage in the culture war to parachurch organizations. We have designated them as the rightful combatants, claiming that churches and denominations should not dirty their hands with the grime of warfare.

The third indicator of evangelical AWOL status in the culture war manifests itself in the failure of evangelicals to develop a strategy for winning. Thankfully, many evangelical warriors are fighting the good fight, such as pro-life advocates and evangelical lawyers fighting for our freedoms in court, and occasionally they win a battle. However, evangelicals are constantly on the defensive, seeking to hold back advances by the left, hoping that they do not gain too much territory. The thought of defeating the left with its ungodly agenda and restoring righteousness to our nation seems almost unthinkable. For example, a return to public schools and universities that promote rational thinking and godly character seems like a whimsical dream that could never actually occur.

Historians attribute the British defeat in the Revolutionary War to widespread malaria, especially among those fighting in the South. Some estimate that by late summer of 1781 malaria had incapacitated as many as half the British forces in the

Tidewater region.[14]

Just as the *Anopheles quadrimaculatus* mosquitoes infected these British forces, the culture that licenses selfishness, now infecting American secular society, has spread to the evangelical church. The resulting corrupted evangelical belief system is sapping it of the strength to fight effectively in the culture war.

In many ways, we parallel the Europeans who allow themselves to be bullied by the Muslim minority. Granted, the left in the United States possesses more resources for doing battle than do the Muslims in Europe. Nonetheless, given the array of resources described above, evangelicals do not need to allow progressives to be the ones always on the offensive, to set the agenda, to establish the rules of the game, to provide the referees, thus assuring that they win.

We can and should be on the offensive. From a historical perspective, this is our country and not theirs. The culture we are seeking to restore is historic American culture. They are the outsiders. They are seeking to impose a foreign culture, and a corrupt one at that—one that is leading to the destruction of America. We have every resource, right, and responsibility to oppose and defeat them. Yet, as with the European majority, we allow progressives to run over us, weakened by the very selfishness-inducing culture that progressives are imposing on secular society.

In his last book, *The Great Evangelical Disaster*, Francis Schaeffer recognized the inclination of evangelicals to be infiltrated by secular ideology and warned:

> We can say the Bible is without mistake and still destroy it if we bend the Scripture by our lives to fit this culture instead of judging the culture by Scripture.... What is the use of evangelicalism seeming to get larger and larger if sufficient numbers of those under the name evangelical no longer hold to that which makes evangelicalism evangelical? ... (I)f we acquiesce, we will no longer be the redeeming salt for our culture.... It makes little difference in the end if Scripture is compromised by theological infiltration or by infiltration from the surrounding culture.... God's Word has many times been allowed to be bent, to conform to the surrounding, passing, changing culture of that moment rather than to stand as the inerrant Word of God judging the form of the world spirit and the surrounding culture of that moment. In the name of the Lord Jesus Christ, may our children and grandchildren not say that such can be said about us.[15]

Unfortunately, Schaeffer's concerns have materialized. Rather than fighting against the 1960s ideology, the evangelical church has adopted its active ingredient. In consequence, it is propagating this cultural disease rather than providing a remedy.

Identifying the Evangelical Disease

Though it may seem far-fetched, the error I speak of is the secular and evangelical commitment to unconditional love and acceptance. I refer to unconditional love and acceptance in the singular because in both secular and evangelical cultures unconditional love and unconditional acceptance are viewed as synonymous.

At first blush this concept sounds like the ultimate expression of goodness. What could possibly be wrong with unconditional love and acceptance? However, even a superficial analysis raises red flags. Accepting a person unconditionally in effect gives him license to do anything he pleases with impunity, which includes selfish behaviors. Because of the human inclination toward selfishness, the person licensed to live selfishly will be inclined to do so.

We see this inclination at work in secular society with the current acceptance of a wide range of behaviors that are harmful to others. For example, acceptance of the transgender biological male in women's sports proves devastating to women who have trained for years to excel in an event, only to be unfairly eliminated by a biological male identifying as a woman.

We witness an evangelical manifestation of unconditional love and acceptance in the more accepting attitude toward divorce. The resulting high divorce rate among evangelicals inflicts devastation on innocent spouses and children.

An analysis of unconditional love and acceptance unearths an array of challenging questions, which is the reason for the book. For example, some may contend that unconditionally accepting the individual does not include accepting behavior that would hurt others. The book addresses that issue, demonstrating that unconditional acceptance in fact does license behavior harmful to others. Some people seek to resolve the moral dilemma created by unconditional acceptance by asserting that they accept the person but not his inappropriate behavior. The book addresses that issue also.

If my concerns are valid, the major role assigned unconditional love and acceptance in both secular and evangelical cultures positions it to inflict substantial damage on secular society and within the evangelical community. Among other negative outcomes, it is eroding secular morality and leaving the evangelical church too sick to fight effectively in the culture war. If the evangelical church would recognize the selfishness-promoting nature of this ideology and restore a biblical belief system, it would regain its vitality, enabling it to fight effectively in the culture war.

Should Evangelicals Engage in This Fight?

For years, evangelicals have debated whether God has called the church to engage in politics. Many have answered in the negative for two reasons. First, they contend that the church's business is not political engagement but preaching the gospel to the lost and discipling the saved. They assert that politics distract from that mission. Second, they argue that politics cannot solve our nation's problems. They insist that only the gospel, lives transformed by the power of God, can rescue our deteriorating society.

This perspective, however, fails to see that the issues at stake in the culture war are not predominantly political but spiritual. Though politics constitutes a major front in that war, ultimately issues such as killing unborn babies, the demise of the family, sexually perverse entertainment, and corrupting the minds of children are spiritual. These issues link politics with morality, and God calls the church to promote morality. Therefore, to perform its mission the church must engage politically.

The legitimacy of the church's engagement becomes even more obvious when we frame the issue in terms of loving our neighbors. The lawyer asked Jesus, "Who is my neighbor?" Likewise, we might ask whether unborn babies about to be slaughtered are our neighbors. If so, Jesus calls us to love them by doing everything possible to rescue them, including involvement in politics. Likewise, loving America's children and young people requires delivering them from educational institutions that corrupt their minds and deprive them of genuine learning. God has assigned us to serve as sources of salt and light, as preservers of morality and propagators of truth. Doing so requires our involvement in the political arena.

Some might contend that believers should meet these responsibilities as individuals or through parachurch organizations and that the church per se should not engage in these pursuits. However, no scriptural basis exists for that position, and to date, it is not working. Only the organized church—denominational and independent churches—possess the numbers and strength to achieve that objective. Limiting our offensive to parachurch organizations is not working and cannot reverse our current cultural corruption.

Our continued pattern of defeat in the culture war warns us that unless we make necessary changes, we will lose the battle to the left as did Israel to Babylon and Germany to Hitler. Therefore, it is essential that we identify the selfishness-licensing ideology that is infecting our secular culture and has now infiltrated the evangelical church. We must understand its destructive nature and provide a biblical alternative. The pages ahead address those issues.

The first step in our study of this selfishness-licensing ideology entails determining why it is so deadly. The next chapter addresses that issue.

Chapter 2: Why Licensing Selfishness Is Deadly

The Power of Culture

This book deals with the ideology that gives license to selfishness. An ideology is just that, simply someone's idea. It gains power, however, when it becomes attached to a culture. Culture wields vast power. Therefore, the ideology that shapes a culture exerts a powerful molding influence on individuals and a society. Ultimately the culture war currently raging in America constitutes a conflict between a culture licensing selfishness and the forces seeking to contain it. Consequently, understanding the power of this ideology requires that we begin by reflecting on the nature and power of culture.

What is culture? Culture consists of the blueprint of reality that resides in the minds of people within a given group. This blueprint constitutes reality as they see and respond to it. Those in a Muslim culture possess a view of reality that influences their beliefs, values, attitudes, and behaviors, consequently shaping virtually everything about the society in which they live. It is likewise with all human beings and their cultures.

Andrew Breitbart made the perceptive observation, "Politics is downstream of culture."16 This assertion, however, only encompasses part of the truth. Virtually everything about a given society is downstream from culture. Culture shapes its religious beliefs, government, judicial approach, morals, entertainment, educational system, and other aspects of societal life. Therefore, a person's culture creates the reality in which he lives, both in terms of his internal perception of the world and the impact of that perception in shaping the society surrounding him. As a result, next to God, culture is arguably the second most powerful force in the universe.

For most people culture determines truth. For most Palestinian men, Islam defines truth. Try to convince them that a woman has a right to wear whatever she wants, and, your chances of success hover right at zero. Likewise, attempts to convince a Kansas college student to consider suicide bombing as a career choice will fail. This difference in perspective does not stem from intellectual ability or genetic makeup. Rather, their culture shapes their perspectives of truth. Had they been switched at birth, they would have embraced the opposite positions. Consequently, for most people, culture exercises the most dominant force in shaping their worldview and lifestyle.

Christians might respond that Scripture and not culture shapes these aspects of their lives. However, as we will see later in the book, even for most Christians, culture exercises a powerful influence in shaping their understanding of life and their behaviors. We will further see that Christian culture can differ significantly from the teachings of Scripture. Consider the Christian cultural perspectives of believers in the South during slavery years.

Confidence that our culture represents truth, the right way to live, results in refusal to identify it as the cause of our current problems. News commentators in their search for the cause of mass shootings look every which way. However, they never seem to consider our culture as the culprit, even though there are many reasons to believe that it is.

Culture possesses additional strength because we are unaware of its influence. Most people, if they think about it at all, conclude that their views stem from rational analysis. People in the West are most prone to this mistake, confident that as products of the Enlightenment they base their views on evidence and reason rather than culture. Culture might shape the beliefs of Muslims or Hindus, but not theirs. However, countless examples reveal that culture also shapes Western thinking and lifestyles. What is their rational justification for saving whales while killing their own babies?

We are not captives of our culture. Human beings possess the intellectual capacity to analyze whether their culture speaks truth and offers wholesome outcomes. However, only a small minority attempts to do so. Most people are too consumed with the activities of daily life, too immobilized by inertia, or too constrained by fear of being different to evaluate their culture objectively and confront its errors. Fewer still are willing to board a Mayflower and sail to a new world to establish their own culture.

Most people prefer life inside their cultural prison rather than to risk the unknowns of the world outside. Beyond that, they assume that their cultural prison walls are constructed of truth, and therefore their culture does not consign them to a prison but rather houses them in a temple.

All Cultures Are Not Created Equal

Multiculturalists claim that all cultures are created equal. Any rational analysis, however, tells us that cultures encouraging suicide bombing, the burning of widows, genocide, or harmful health habits get low scores in engendering the good life. No culture is perfect, but some do a significantly better job of producing a wholesome environment than others.

Or let's evaluate culture from a different perspective. I mentioned earlier that culture consists of the blueprint of reality imprinted on our mind. However, reality has an objective existence outside of our minds. The more closely a given culture's internal blueprint of reality corresponds to actual reality, the better it will work. For example, a communist culture does not work as well as one embracing capitalism because the communist view of human nature does not correspond as closely as a capitalist one to the realities related to how human beings function.

What difference does cultural influence make? Let me illustrate.

The National Football League (NFL) consists of two conferences, the American Football Conference (AFC) and National Football Conference (NFC). Imagine that the NFL scheduled an NFC team to play against an AFC opponent in every game. Now imagine that they tilted each field 5 degrees and required AFC teams always to play uphill while NFC teams played downhill. This arrangement would make everything a little harder for AFC teams and easier for the NFC teams. AFC teams might win a few games, but most of the time they would lose. AFC fans, tired of losing, would stop coming, and franchise income would decline, while NFC teams would become rich from growing attendances. Though AFC teams may stay in business, they would always be second-rate. All these results would stem from a mere 5-degree tilt of the field.

As with these football conferences, the tilt imposed by a superior culture will likewise promote success. People living in more wholesome cultures will enjoy advantages such as increased affluence, safety, order, education, sanitation, justice, and many other benefits. Tilting the cultural field 10% or 20% makes outcomes even more pronounced.

Characteristic that Produces Cultural Greatness

What core characteristic produces an optimal culture—provides the most favorable cultural tilt?

Fifteenth-century sailors on long voyages developed symptoms such as lethargy, spots on their skin, spongy and bleeding gums, tooth loss, jaundice, fever, and finally death. They had contracted scurvy, a disease resulting from a lack of vitamin C (ascorbic acid), contained in fresh fruits and vegetables.

Just as the physical body requires vitamin C for survival and health, so human psyches and societies need agape for survival and health. Jesus made this human need for agape apparent when He mandated its production in the First Commandment, the Second Commandment, and the New Commandment. Agape production brings health both to the one displaying agape and the one receiving it. The person producing agape enjoys a wholesome and happy life, and his doing so promotes good relationships and a healthy society.

The Nature of Agape

Exactly what is agape? Greek has several words that define different types of love whereas English is limited to one. This limitation tends to promote confusion making it important that when we use the term "love" we have an accurate definition in mind. *Agape* refers to intentions and actions beneficial to others. Some define agape as the love of God. Certainly, God displays agape, but Jesus taught that even less than exemplary human beings can display agape. He asserted in Matthew 5:46, "For if you love those who love you, what reward do you have? Do not even the tax collectors do the same?" Here Jesus tells us that even tax collectors, a term He is not using with a complimentary connotation in this context, at times display agape, the Greek word used in that passage. Therefore, agape does not possess some sort of supernatural connotation but merely refers to seeking the benefit of others. Evangelicals especially tend to defined agape as unconditional love. In a later chapter, we will discover the problems with that definition. It is best just to understand agape simply as intentions and actions having the objective of benefiting others.

The term love in English versions of the New Testament is usually a translation of agape. Agape is the word used in the First and Second Commandments regarding our responsibility to love God and our neighbor, and for the New Commandment, which calls believers to love one another. Mention of love in this book will refer to agape unless otherwise indicated. Jesus described agape using the story of the Good Samaritan, a foreigner who helped a man beaten by robbers and left for dead. The Samaritan expressed agape by binding up this man's wounds, loading him on his donkey, taking him to an inn, caring for him, and promising the innkeeper to cover additional expenses.

Philia describes emotional love, which covers a broad range of feelings from friendship to romance. *Eros* denotes sexual love.

Let me clarify the difference between agape and philia. Jesus calls us to display agape toward our enemies. We cannot make ourselves feel warmly (philia) toward enemies, but we can seek their benefit (agape). A coworker snubs you and treats you rudely. Try as you might, you cannot conjure up warm feelings (philia) toward this coworker. You learn, however, that she is about to get fired because she lacks understanding of an aspect of her job that you know well and could teach her. Despite your negative feelings (lack of philia), you offer to teach her that skill (display agape).

Because historically love has been so powerfully related to romance, when English speaking people hear the word love, philia, feeling-type love, rather than agape, action-type love, tends to come to mind. Since the 1960s culture, with its focus on feelings, has become dominant in our society, this tendency to associate love with feelings has grown even stronger. Even when specifically discussing agape, people tend to veer away from will and action toward feelings in their meaning, causing confusion.

Agape is a relational term. God designed us to live in multiple relational settings such as families, organizations, and societies, and above all, in a relationship with Him. Cultures that promote agape within these relationships breed success.

Expressions of Agape

We express agape in two forms: morality and grace. A culture that values and promotes these qualities will produce significant quantities of agape, which will engender success.

Morality

Morality entails giving others what we owe them, that is, dealing with them fairly. It comprises the foundational expression of agape. We are obligated to do at least that much for them. In Romans 13:9-

10, the apostle Paul teaches that agape includes this moral dimension:

> For the commandments, "You shall not commit adultery, you shall not murder, you shall not steal, you shall not covet," and any other commandment, are summed up in this word: "You shall love your neighbor as yourself."

Our moral obligations cover a lot of territory. Our roles as spouse, parent, child, employer, employee, citizen, fellow believer, neighbor, and friend all carry with them moral obligations. It is likewise with business dealings.

It is easy to understand why morality, giving others what you owe them, embodies an expression of agape. Being fair and honest certainly benefits others more than robbing or cheating them. We might ask, however, how maintaining some of God's moral standards, such as marriage as opposed to cohabitation, are expressions of agape.

First, they embody agape because we are called to show agape toward God. Keeping His commandments achieves that objective.

However, keeping God's moral standards also produces agape because they provide the greatest benefit to others. That outcome is not always evident to us. It is obvious, however, in most cases. For example, cohabitation fails to provide the lifetime commitment commensurate with sexual intimacy. Thus, even when sexual relations are consensual, failure to make that commitment takes something very precious from persons without giving them due compensation. This arrangement also robs children born into that relationship of the stable home-life parents owe them and marriage provides.

Morality serves as the gears that make society work. Government, business, family, educational institutions, and interaction between neighbors and friends all depend on the exercise of morality. For example, it is virtually impossible to maintain a good relationship with a person who lies or steals. In the absence of morality, relationships turn chaotic and societies disintegrate.

Grace

While morality comprises the foundational component of agape, grace constitutes its highest expression. Morality gives others what we owe them, while grace gives what we do not owe. Your neighbor is sick, so you mow his lawn. Since you have no moral obligation to do so, this action displays grace. The cross exhibited history's greatest expression of grace. Christ died to pay for our sins, providing forgiveness, eternal life, and countless other blessings He did not owe us.

While morality serves as the gears that make society work, grace provides the oil that lubricates those gears, preventing overheating and reducing friction. If we were all perfect, we could function just fine solely on the basis of morality. Human flaws make the oil of grace necessary. Overdrawing our checking account results in brutal fees of $35 or so for each bounced check. Our agreement with the bank gives it the moral right to charge that fee. Then banks introduced overdraft protection, the oil of grace applied to financial gears. Grace is the overdraft protection God extends to us and that He calls us to extend to family, friends, and even enemies.

It is wrong to extend grace at the expense of morality, e.g. to neglect paying my electric bill in order to give to a charity. Doing so constitutes stealing from the electric company. Agape requires that we meet moral obligations first. Extending grace at the expense of morality may seem noble. Ultimately, however, it leads to societal breakdown, which hurts everyone. A judge released a gang member who then murdered four people. If we display grace at the expense of morality, relational gears will jam and leave a puddle of the oil of grace on the floor.

Since grace requires giving, someone must pay for it. God did not provide grace, forgiveness for our sins, by sweeping them under the carpet. That would have been unjust—grace at the expense of morality. Rather, He paid for them at the cross. The Good Samaritan's display of grace cost him effort, time, and financial resources. In our society, people want to extend grace by requiring someone else to pay for it. That is not grace but robbery.

Agape as a Lifestyle

Often we limit our perspective on agape to being nice to people. "He is a loving person" means that he displays kindness, especially to needy people. Agape includes that but vastly more.

Jesus when queried about the greatest commandment responded, "And you shall love the Lord your God with all your heart and with all your soul and with all your mind and with all your strength." (Mar 12:30) Note that Jesus commanded us to love the Lord with all of every aspect of our being. The apostle Paul reveals the all-encompassing scope of agape by instructing, "Let all *that* you *do* be done with love." (1 Corinthians 16:14) Our every thought, attitude, word, and act should reflect agape.

Combining the teachings of Christ and Paul, Scripture is commanding us to use every component of our lives and every behavior to produce agape. In other words, for the believer, agape production should be an all-consuming objective that results in a lifestyle characterized by agape. Success of an individual and culture requires an approach to life that makes benefitting others our primary value, an orientation that we live out in every aspect of our existence.

Why Agape Produces Success

Agape produces success because God designed human beings to function as agape-producing organisms. Qualities that we identify as "humane," the essence of being human, such as kindness and mercy, constitute expressions of agape. Therefore, practicing them makes us fully human—results in our functioning according to God's design. When we operate our lives according to the Manufacturer's design by producing agape, they work optimally and we enjoy success.

For example, agape promotes well-being in the major components of our existence:

- **Agape optimizes relational well-being.** A marriage characterized by agape, which includes qualities such as fidelity, patience, consideration, responsibility, and compassion, is far more functional, meaningful, and enduring than one characterized by the opposite qualities. Likewise, an employer/employee relationship in which both parties consistently function based on agape toward each other will produce harmony, mutual benefit, stability, and success.

- **Agape optimizes emotional well-being.** It does so for both the person expressing it and the one receiving it. Morality, fidelity, responsibility, and other expressions of agape eliminate guilt and create a clear conscience, a sense of integrity, and the resulting peace. It also minimizes discord, producing an emotionally healthy environment.

- **Agape optimizes physical well-being.** Optimizing relational and emotional health promotes physical health. In addition, agape requires that we exercise good stewardship of our bodies so that we can use them to minister to others.

- **Agape optimizes financial well-being.** Agape calls us to be good stewards of our finances since money becomes a major means of expressing agape. Loving choices also tend to be less expensive. Consider the cost of a DUI.

- **Agape optimizes societal well-being.** Society constitutes a network of relationships. Optimizing those relationships through the production of agape generates health in society as a whole. A society committed to agape would reduce divorce, crime, drunk-driving, and a host of other very expensive, disruptive, and painful societal maladies.

Earlier I made the point that a culture, a blueprint of reality in one's mind, that most closely conforms to external, genuine reality engenders the greatest success. Since God created us to produce agape, life works optimally when the culture in our minds assigns it the dominant role. We are happier and better off, those to whom we express agape receive benefit, and society as a whole works better.

Optimizing Agape Production Is Difficult

Though, as we have just observed, agape production is highly beneficial, it is also demanding. We might liken agape production to swimming upstream against the current while selfishness is much like floating downstream with the current. In other words, agape production is challenging while being selfish comes naturally—the spontaneous product of our fallen nature.

If it were easy to produce agape, perhaps we might do an adequate job despite the licensing of selfishness. However, because agape production is difficult, licensing selfishness is tantamount to making the current opposing agape production much swifter, making it substantially more difficult to swim upstream and much more tempting to go downstream with the flow of the current of selfishness.

The fact that agape production is difficult raises two questions: why do we produce it and how do we produce it.

Why We Produce Agape

Several factors motivate us to produce agape. As believers, the Holy Spirit prompts and empowers us to display agape. However, as a helper, He does not force us. That becomes evident from the fact that we still have the option to be selfish, one we tend to exercise at times, even as believers. A second motivator resides in the benefits agape produces mentioned above. The prospects of better relationships, financial benefits, and emotional well-being make agape a good choice,

However, at times temptations toward selfishness overpower our desire to produce it. At those times we are confronted with a third motivation: the authority and commandments of God. For the believer, agape production is not optional but mandatory. When other motivations fail, recognition that God holds us accountable to produce agape becomes an essential motivation.

How We Produce Agape

We produce agape through the intentional management of all of our resources to achieve that objective. Peter commands: "As each has received a gift, use it to serve one another, as good stewards of God's varied grace..." (1 Peter 4:10) That gift embodies all of the resources God has assigned to us: time, health, natural and spiritual gifts, education, financial resources, position, influence, network of relationships, etc. A steward in biblical times functioned as a manager, overseeing the owner's resources. Likewise, God has assigned us to manage all our resources in order to optimize agape production.

The human capability to manage intentionally to produce agape reflects our creation in the image of God. God is intentional. He is a self-conscious Being driven by purpose. God is also loving, that is, He employs His intentional nature to produce agape. Likewise, our creation in His image gives us the capability to manage our lives to intentionally produce agape. Previously we saw that God's authority provided us with the *responsibility* to produce agape. Here we see that our creation in the image of God provides us with the *capability* to produce agape.

This intentional management requires engagement of our mind and will. God designed animals to function spontaneously—based on instinct. A squirrel does not ponder what he must do today to fulfill his purpose for existence as a squirrel. He merely follows his instincts, and they provide the guidance and motivation to spontaneously fulfill his function as a squirrel. Not so with human beings. Successful living requires employing our mind to determine the most effective courses of action and employing our will to implement the guidance of the mind. Optimal functioning in all areas of life requires this purpose-driven management process employing the mind and will. That includes agape production.

In Philippians 1:9-10, the apostle Paul indicates that we need to employ our minds to produce agape by writing, "And it is my prayer that your love may abound more and more, with knowledge and all discernment..." Agape production requires "knowledge and all discernment," which only our minds can supply. We derive much knowledge and discernment from Scripture, which requires that we use our minds in reading, understanding, and applying it. Agape production also requires the use of our minds in gathering facts and analyzing situations in order to know how best to benefit others.

Our feelings, the subjective aspect of our personality, seek to direct our lives. However, God did not design our feelings to function as the human GPS. Most of the time they guide us toward destructive decisions. They prompt us to eat too much, make unkind comments, and spend irresponsibly. Usually they lead us in selfish directions.

The will functions as referee between the mind's guidance toward agape production and our desires that lead toward selfishness. Loving behaviors often require the exercise of the will to overcome selfish cravings. While our mind votes against a second helping of tiramisu, our emotions insist that we will not survive till morning without it. The will is stuck with the task of rejecting the perverse demands of our desires and instead implementing guidance of the mind toward agape.

Even when our feelings seem to be guiding us in loving directions, we must give our minds veto power, since loving feelings do not always lead toward actions that benefit others. A friend craves double chocolate suicide cake. I will show my love by baking him one. However, he happens to be diabetic. Consequently, even when feelings seek to show kindness, agape production requires that we give our mind ultimate authority and employ our will to implement the directions of our mind.

Maximizing agape requires that we do our best in every pursuit. Solomon taught, "Whatever your hand finds to do, do it with your might...." (Ecclesiastes 9:10) Paul instructed, "Whatever you do, work heartily, as for the Lord and not for men...." (Colossians 3:23) Paul commands, "Therefore, my beloved brothers, be steadfast, immovable, always abounding in the work of the Lord, knowing that in the Lord your labor is not in vain." (1 Corinthians 15:58) Maximum agape production requires that we strive to be the best student, employee, spouse, parent, and friend possible. Doing so demands full engagement of our energies in executing these tasks.

Agape often calls us to do hard things. For example, it requires that couples work out differences even when loving feelings are gone—when powerful negative feelings have replaced them. It demands that we invest long hours to finish a project and do it well. It can require that we apologize and ask for forgiveness. We might need to confront an unpleasant situation, a task most of us dread. Consequently, displaying agape often demands courage, discipline, and endurance.

Adversaries of Agape Production

Producing agape is especially demanding because powerful forces prompt us to produce selfishness rather than agape. Christians often label these adversaries of agape as the world, the flesh, and the devil.

Sometimes Scripture uses the Greek term "cosmos," translated "world," to refer to secular culture. Earlier we discussed the power of culture. Human cultures often promote selfishness and militate against agape production. Our current secular culture, the "world" confronting us, provides us with the license to live selfishly, increasing the incentive to adopt selfish values and behaviors. It exerts this influence through entertainment media, educational institutions, and elsewhere.

This environment makes agape production more challenging.

In Scripture, "the flesh" refers to the inclination of our fallen nature toward self-gratification. This tendency runs diametrically counter to agape. Scripture teaches that believers possess a dual nature. This reality surfaces in Paul's dealing with the Corinthians.

> And I, brethren, could not speak to you as to spiritual men, but as to men of flesh, as to infants in Christ. I gave you milk to drink, not solid food; for you were not yet able to receive it. Indeed, even now you are not yet able, for you are still fleshly. For since there is jealousy and strife among you, are you not fleshly, and are you not walking like mere men? For when one says, "I am of Paul," and another, "I am of Apollos," are you not mere men? (1 Corinthians 3:1-4 NASB)

This passage reveals that even believers possess the potential for selfishness and that at times those tendencies gain the upper hand.

The book of 1 Corinthians provides us with many examples of the power of the flesh at work in that church. Even with the ministry of the Holy Spirit empowering us to produce agape, fighting off the demands of the flesh constitutes a continuing battle.

In Ephesians 6:11-12, Paul warns us about the devil:

> Put on the whole armor of God, that you may be able to stand against the schemes of the devil. For we do not wrestle against flesh and blood, but against the rulers, against the authorities, against the cosmic powers over this present darkness, against the spiritual forces of evil in the heavenly places.

In the Book of Job, we find him bringing destruction and death on everything associated with Job. When God allows him leeway, apparently he has the power to create profound misery. It also appears that he possesses the potential to place temptations before our eyes and arouse wicked thoughts in our minds. Peter warns that "your adversary the devil prowls around like a roaring lion, seeking someone to devour." (1 Peter 5:8) He knows our weaknesses and attacks us where we are most vulnerable. His work makes producing agape a struggle, one we can win but a struggle nonetheless.

God's Answers to Adversaries of Agape

God provides us with resources for countering the assaults of the world, the flesh, and the devil. These resources do not end the battle, but they do give us the capacity to win each struggle confronting us.

The Lord makes provision for us to counteract the pressures of the world. As believers, we live not only in the material world but also in the spiritual world, which envelops us in a spiritual culture. Therefore, we find ourselves simultaneously living in two spheres of existence.

The material world continues to push its agenda on us, making it a struggle to maintain a spiritual focus. However, as we read and meditate on Scripture, spend time in prayer, and fellowship with other believers, the spiritual cosmos becomes the dominant force in our lives. When the spiritual sphere gains dominance, its influence results in optimal agape production.

To counter the flesh, God provides every believer with a new nature that possesses an inclination toward agape. The old nature continues to promote selfishness, but this new nature pushes back against these selfish messages.

The Lord also empowers us to overcome the work of the devil. When we received Christ, the Holy Spirit takes up residence within us, giving us the power to defeat Satan. While Satan promotes selfishness, the presence and power of the Holy Spirit encourages and enables us to produce agape.

We see, then, that agape production is hard work and at times a fierce battle, but one that God empowers us to win. Nonetheless, life consists of an ongoing struggle between our pursuit of agape production and the resistance and temptation of selfishness.

Agape, Selfishness, and Cultural Success

The Devastation a Selfishness Producing Culture

This struggle between agape production and the lure of selfishness returns us to the issue of culture. We have identified culture as wielding powerful influence over society. We have identified agape as the characteristic that produces success. Therefore, a culture characterized by agape produces optimal societal health and success.

Selfishness comprises the opposite of agape. Agape seeks to benefit others. Selfishness pursues benefit for self even at the expense of others. The ideology that licenses selfishness comprises a deadly strain of selfishness that assigns to itself total authority to pursue its own desires by denying the personhood of others.

Since agape comprises the characteristic that promotes societal health and success, and since selfishness constitutes its diametric opposite, it becomes evident why a culture that licenses selfishness imposes a devastating impact on individuals and society.

We find an illustration of the lethal impact of selfishness as we consider the role of the cardiovascular system in the human body.

Just as culture influences virtually every aspect of life, likewise the cardiovascular system reaches almost every aspect of the human body and exerts a profound influence. Perhaps its most significant role resides in delivering oxygen to the cells of the body, which is essential for providing them with life, energy, and the capacity to produce new cells. Oxygen is to the human body what agape is to the human soul and society. As we have seen, it comprises the entity essential for the wellbeing of human existence.

The presence of excessive carbon monoxide in an environment impedes the flow of oxygen. When the blood passes through the lungs, the hemoglobin in the blood attracts the oxygen present there, taking it on and carrying it around to the rest of the body, where it is released to provide life and energy. However, if when the blood passes through the lungs carbon monoxide is present, the hemoglobin has an even greater attraction for it than for oxygen. In response, the carbon monoxide takes up the space in the hemoglobin normally occupied by oxygen. Consequently, the blood cannot absorb that oxygen and distribute it throughout the body. This soon leads to sickness and ultimately to death.

Selfishness is the carbon monoxide of culture. It tends to displace agape, robbing individuals and society of agape's lifegiving properties. Because of our human fallen nature, we have a greater natural attraction to selfishness than we do to agape. Therefore, a culture giving license to selfishness creates its buildup in excessive concentrations. This condition chokes out agape and inflicts cultural sickness and death.

These realities demonstrate that at the core of our human existence resides the battle between agape and selfishness. Ultimately life is about the struggle to produce agape which requires that we overcome our inclinations to behave selfishly. Individual and societal health and success are determined by how well we do in that fight. People are strongly influenced by their cultural environment. One that encourages agape production will help them overcome selfishness and maintain lifestyles characterized substantially by agape.

America was great initially because a substantial contingent of its founding generations embraced a biblical form of Christianity, which imposed agape on American culture as a primary characteristic. America's decline in virtually every area is resulting from a culture that grants license to selfishness.

The Devastation of Unconditional Love and Acceptance

Since agape produces cultural success, it may seem that unconditional love and acceptance would comprise the ultimate success-producing characteristic. A culture characterized by unconditional love should produce maximum success.

The ideology of unconditional love and acceptance has gained prominence and power in secular and evangelical cultures for precisely that reason. A superficial analysis does suggest that it embodies the ultimate virtue. In the previous chapter, however, I provided some preliminary indicators that unconditional love and acceptance does not comprise the virtuous nature that it suggests at first blush. Among other considerations, this book includes an account of an experiment performed by a leading psychologist designed to show the merits of unconditional love and acceptance. Instead, the outcome exposes the devastating influence of this ideology. Though it may seem counterintuitive, the promotion of unconditional love and acceptance results in the licensing of selfishness rather than the advancement of agape.

America can be made great again only if we restore our agape-promoting culture. That will require, however, that we stop giving license to selfishness.

Achieving that will first require that we understand the secular ideology that has led to the promotion of selfishness and has infiltrated the evangelical church, making the church part of the problem rather than the solution. Restoring America requires that we first cast the beam out of our own eye before seeking to remove the speck from the eye of secular culture.

Licensing selfishness started in secular society. Therefore, we will begin our examination of this ideology by exploring its secular roots. Then we will consider its psychological form. That will lead us to its infiltration into the contemporary evangelical belief system.

SECTION TWO
IDEOLOGY OF SELFISHNESS

This book contends that a culture that gives people a license to be selfish is destroying our nation. This section explains that this culture is rooted in the ideology imposed on our society beginning in the 1960s. It describes its core characteristics and destructive nature.

Chapter 1: Paving the Way for Our Current Culture

Culture exercises a powerful influence over the individual and society, and a culture characterized by agape produces success. America's traditional Christian culture promoted agape production, which shaped our values and behaviors. This agape-creating culture promoted success in every dimension of American life.

However, in the 1960s, a new irrational, feelings-oriented ideology took our nation by storm. Since then it has permeated every dimension of American existence. It replaced our agape-producing, Christian-oriented culture with selfishness-generating concepts and values.

This development prompts the question, why would America replace our successful Christian culture with an irrational one that invokes chaos and decline? Two factors opened the door to this new orientation.

The Advent of Materialism

Charles Darwin published his *On the Origins of Species* in 1859. His theory of evolution led secular scientists to conclude that they no longer needed God to explain our existence. In response, they embraced a view of the universe consisting solely of matter and energy, commonly known as materialism.

The fact that a majority of secular scientists embraced materialism created the impression that a person committed to science necessarily believes the materialist perspective. In other words, our society adopted the perspective that science and materialism were synonymous.

Since materialism excludes the existence of all nonmaterial aspects of the universe, it rejects Christianity, at least in its biblical form. This rejection of Christianity became the dominant position within the academic community. This resulted in the branding of Christians and others not embracing materialism as uneducated and unscientific.

Materialism became the cornerstone of contemporary liberalism. Its hallmarks include the rejection of Christianity and its values, a naturalistic explanation for the universe, development of morals and values based solely on human perceptions, use of reason and the scientific method unaided by Scripture as a basis for determining truth, and the confidence that these tools in the hands of big government can lead us to utopia.

Deficiencies of Materialism

However, materialism's claim to be scientific ultimately began to unravel. For example, the discovery of the overwhelming complexities of a living cell reveals that the evolutionary mechanism of time plus chance plus natural selection could not possibly explain its existence. A series of videos created by the Discovery Institute entitled Science_Uprising divulges the many weaknesses in the materialist explanation for the development of life.[17]

Despite overwhelming evidence that discredits the materialist position rationally, materialists continue to cling to their perspective, apparently driven by a desire for a universe devoid of God. Consequently, materialism does not represent science per se but constitutes an "-ism," an ideology, a belief system.

Materialism also became discredited by its failure to live up to its promises. It asserted that through science and education, materialism would ultimately bring in utopia. World War I, World War II, and the Cold War threat of nuclear annihilation revealed that materialism was moving humanity in a negative direction.

Americans also began to reject materialism because of its dehumanizing tenets. For example, it contends that:

- Humans consist only of molecules and energy— depriving them of a soul.
- Humans differ from animals only in degree and not in kind.
- Humans are biological machines with no free will.
- Humans lack any capacity for genuine dignity and love.
- Human beings possess no unique value, thus eradicating any moral implication of Hitler's genocide or Stalin's mass murderers.
- Aging and other forces leave many human beings as liabilities to be eliminated.
- A universe devoid of God leaves humans without help beyond themselves.
- Humans are temporal creatures and therefore have no eternal hope.

The materialist assertion that humans only consist of molecules and energy, biological machines, renders human beings incapable of producing genuine agape. A machine cannot love. It also undermines any reason for displaying agape, since persons only consist of matter and energy and therefore have no unique value. Why should a person give of himself for an organized heap of matter and energy?

This system devoid of agape had little public appeal. Americans may have believed that it was intellectually valid, but it was totally unsatisfying at an emotional level. As a result, though it has been taught in public schools and universities for decades, it has not significantly eroded the American belief in God. A recent Gallup poll reveals that 87% of Americans still believe in God. [18]

Rejection of Materialism

Academics also began to question whether reason (scientific analysis) could provide knowledge with absolute certainty. What appears to be a solid wall consists primarily of empty space. What, then, is reality? Can science reveal its essence? Our inability to draw concrete conclusions regarding a concrete wall calls into question the capacity of reason to establish certainty regarding more abstract issues such as the purpose of life.

These concerns prompted some intellectuals, those who shape culture, to reject materialism's employment of reason to determine reality. Having rejected Christianity, and now having assessed reason to be inadequate, intellectuals resorted to subjectivity rather than objectivity as the basis for determining reality. That is, they embraced feelings over facts and reason as comprising the valid approach to life. They concluded that immediate experience and the related feelings comprised the only means of achieving knowledge with certainty. My intellectual conclusions about the wall may be wrong, but I can be certain of my subjective experience of it if I run into it headfirst. This perception of reality based on feelings rather than reason is by definition irrational.

Consequently, beginning in the 1960s an ideology invaded America that viewed emotions, feelings, subjective experience as the only reliable means of determining reality and guiding our lives. This commitment to the subjective found expression in the hippie slogan "If it feels good, do it." As noted earlier, God did not design our feelings to function as a GPS for our lives, and therefore the adoption of an ideology assigning emotions to that role has spelled disaster. Nonetheless, this irrational, feelings approach to life comprises the cultural force driving America's current progressive movement and American secular society in general.

We see, then, that materialism led America to the rejection of Christianity, but being unsatisfying itself, prompted the rejection of objective reason and its replacement by an irrational, feelings-based approach to life.

Weapons of Cultural Transformation

A second force that opened the door to America's abandonment of our Christian culture for our current feelingsoriented, irrational culture resides in the development of technologies that possess the power to propagate irrationality.

Technological Developments

The 1950s brought us the small, cheap transistor radio. As a result, instead of families gathering around the living room radio, kids had their own radios that they listened to in their own rooms. This enabled the propagation of a teen music culture largely out of reach of parental supervision. Music exercises a powerful influence in molding culture. Think about its impact in spawning the hippie culture. Therefore, the transistor radio provided an avenue for cultural transformation.

The advent of television provided another means of injecting cultural values through news, sitcoms, and other programming. One survey revealed that Americans over two years of age watch television 34 hours per week on average.[19]

These technological developments were quickly followed by the VHS player, the Walkman, the DVD player, the Internet, iTunes, the iPod, video games, smartphones, the iPad and other tablets, Netflix and Amazon movies, social media, and almost countless variations of the above. Though movies had been around for a long time, these outlets vastly expanded their reach. Also, new technology such as ultra-high-definition, CGI (computer-generated imagery), and increased sound quality substantially enhanced the power of movies to influence minds and emotions.

Those controlling these technological developments exercised vast power to shape American culture. Children and teenagers were especially vulnerable having more time to use these media, possessing more malleable minds, and being more influenced by peer pressure. Some young people stream music into their ears all night while they sleep.

Power to Promote the Irrational

These technological developments exercise power not only because they provide access to the minds and hearts of Americans, but also because they possessed a unique capacity to sell irrational concepts. Neil Postman's book *Amusing Ourselves to Death*, explains this power to implant irrational ideas. Postman asserted that "photography and writing ... do not inhabit the same universe of discourse."[20] While language demands rational engagement, pictures resist it.

> Language, of course, is the medium we use to challenge, dispute, and cross-examine what comes into view, what is on the surface. The words "true" and "false" come from the universe of language, and no other. When applied to a photograph, the question, Is it true? means only, Is this a reproduction of a real slice of spacetime? If the answer is "Yes," there are no grounds for argument, for it makes no sense to disagree with an unfaked photograph. The photograph itself makes no arguable propositions, makes no extended and unambiguous commentary. It offers no assertions to refute, so it is not refutable.[21]

Consequently, writing and other verbal communication promote rational analysis, while pictures tend to bypass our rational processes, embedding unfiltered concepts directly into our minds.

Many of the technological advances described above communicate through pictures and allow pictures to be transmitted more easily and effectively. Therefore, they exercise vast capacities to inject irrational concepts into the minds of Americans. Postman saw television as a special threat to rational discourse because it employed pictures and also because it invaded our homes, becoming the primary conveyor of culture.[22]

Not only pictures but all forms of non-rational communication possess the power to bypass rational analysis and insert messages directly into our minds. Virtually all entertainment fits this description. Though music lyrics, movie plots, and television entertainment use words, they present those words in contexts that elude rational analyzes. We listen to music and watch sitcoms and movies for entertainment, not education. Consequently, the listener turns off his analytical mind, absorbing the message without questioning its validity. We would reject many of these concepts if presented in a rational context.

Few if any young people analyzed the lyrics of John Lennon's "Imagine" to ponder the truth of its claims that Heaven and Hell do not exist or that globalism would eliminate killing. Consequently, these concepts embedded themselves directly into their belief system. The vast numbers of times young people listen to a popular song significantly increases this power to embed its message. Beyond that, the emotional impact of music implants the lyrics even more indelibly into the psyche. All of us remember the lyrics of songs from decades ago and even experience the emotions attached to them.

The concepts conveyed by these lyrics and other verbal messages presented in non-rational contexts attach themselves to the listener's worldview without rational processing, imposing related values, attitudes, and behaviors. Beginning in the 1960s, this non-rational input began transforming the culture of American youth from an objective, rational perspective to a subjective, irrational one.

Progressive Cultural Control

Progressive Control of Technology

Progressives recognized the potential of these technologies as weapons of mass indoctrination and employed them in the propagation of the irrational 1960s ideology. They used these technologies to promote sexual promiscuity, homosexuality, anti-American and anti-Christian perspectives, antiauthoritarian views, and violence.

Why did conservatives not adopt these tools to propagate their message? Maybe because they are conservative. Instead, they allowed a relatively small contingent of progressives to gain control of these outlets and to impose their culture on America while conservatives looked on and complained.

Conservatives do utilize talk radio. Progressives cannot gain traction in this arena because, as Postman's theory explains, talk radio uses words, a medium that invites rational analysis. Therefore, progressive ideas, which are largely irrational, do not play well in this medium. However, talk radio has made only limited inroads since virtually everyone watches progressive-oriented television and movies while talk radio attracts only a predominantly conservative audience. Fox News and a fledgling Christian/conservative movie industry also provide an alternative to the progressive message. These conservative conduits, however, are no match for the dominant outlets controlled by the left.

The Internet constitutes one means of communication in which conservatives have had a more equitable representation. However, the left continues to pursue ways to control that medium such as limiting conservative access to social media. The censoring of conservative messages by social media becomes more flagrant with each passing day.

Progressive Dominance in Education

Progressive control of educational institutions, especially higher education, has provided a powerful platform for imposing a non-rational culture on malleable minds. Though teaching is a verbal medium, the left is able to use educational institutions to propagate non-rational ideas because teachers, for the most part, are older, hold positions of almost dictatorial authority, have imposing academic credentials, are often protected by tenure, and are sheltered from scrutiny by the walls of the academy. They also use a variety of tactics to prevent conservatives from presenting their positions and challenging progressive ones. Beyond that, they enforce politically correct speech and behavior on campus with dictatorial authority.

In his book *Slouching Towards Gomorrah*, the late Robert Bork described "the rejection of the very idea of rationality" by the academic community.[23] Bork referred to "the astounding claim that rationality itself is neither possible nor legitimate...." These academics assert "that what counts as rationality is socially constructed, that there are different ways of knowing, which means that reality has no stable content, not even in principle."[24] Bork wrote of "the denial that rationality, now routinely derided as 'logocentrism,' is legitimate or perhaps even possible...."[25]

John R. Searle reports that problems in academia are confined...

> not just to the content of the curriculum but to the very conception of rationality, truth, objectivity, and reality that have been taken for granted in higher education, as they have been taken for granted in our civilization at large.[26]

The promotion of irrationality in educational institutions serves to divide universities into two separate compartments: those representing the materialism of traditional liberalism and those dominated by progressives. Both of these contingents are in agreement in their rejection of Christianity and its values. They differ, however, in their commitment to reason versus feelings, materialism versus progressivism. Materialists teach subjects that require empirical content and reason such as physics, chemistry, engineering, and medical research. Advocates of progressivism are found teaching majors such as such as social studies, philosophy, history, counseling psychology, journalism, and education. Michael Barone's book *Hard America, Soft America*, recognizes this dichotomy, hard America consisting of fields requiring rational thought while soft America observes no such constraint. He reports: "Americans at 18 have for many years scored lower on standardized tests than 18-year-olds in other advanced countries."[27] He attributes this outcome to the predominant influence of soft America over our educational system.[28] The progressive perspectives of soft America have dominated our news and entertainment media, our judicial system, government bureaucracy, and educational institutions.

These platforms have allowed those advancing an irrational perspective to shape our culture and view of reality.

The Bottom Line

Progressives possess almost sole proprietorship of the channels that influence young people, controlling the music industry, television news and entertainment, movies, social media, and schools. Consequently, as the conservative element of society ages and the progressive-indoctrinated younger generation emerges, the irrational concepts of the left gain increasingly greater traction in American society.

The next chapter describes the nature of this irrational ideology that progressives have sold to America.

Chapter 2: Cultural Invasion

This chapter describes the American invasion by the progressive ideology in the 1960s. As we will see, this ideology issues a license to live selfishly, the antithesis of agape. As a result, it is imposing corruption and destruction on American culture. Future sections will consider the companion psychological and theological perspectives promoting selfishness.

The Hippie Movement

America was invaded in the 1960s, not militarily, but culturally. Though many Americans continued to embrace Christian culture, the new one constituted the cutting edge, ultimately becoming America's dominant ideology. The generally accepted perspective that America has now entered a post-Christian era is correct. Though trends during the 1950s paved the way, the actual American Cultural Revolution began in earnest in the mid-1960s.

Mention of the hippie movement conjures up scenes of the British Invasion with the Beatles' tour of America in 1964-65, the Summer of Love in San Francisco in 1967, the protest at the Democratic National Convention in Chicago in 1968, and Woodstock in rural New York in 1969. It brings to mind unconventional dress and hairstyles, rock music, drugs, the "sexual revolution," and communal living. It also calls to remembrance personalities such as Timothy Leary on the East Coast, Ken Kesey on the West Coast, Norman Mailer, who provided literary inspiration to the movement, and Herbert Marcuse, who provided its intellectual impetus. Its popularity manifested itself in the Summer of Love attendance of 100,000 and Woodstock drawing about 400,000.

The concepts that drove the hippie movement form our current cultural orientation. Though cultural observers divide Americans into six generations, the hippie ideology has imposed its influence on them all. In fact, it shapes virtually every major theme in post-Christian America, our current culture merely reflecting the 1960s culture come of age. Most Americans sense an emotional connection with the hippie movement—as representing *their* culture. Consequently, they view it favorably—young people advocating for love instead of war, with various cool happenings such as Woodstock representing "the good old days."

The concepts comprising the hippie counter-cultural movement, however, were not innocent or altruistic. Rather, our examination will reveal that the hippie movement, "the love generation," in reality spawned and propagated a culture of selfishness.

Hippie Influence on the American Culture

The hippie movement was inspired by progressive academics that had gained influence in American universities. For example, Herbert Marcuse, a major figure of the Frankfurt School, provided substantial impetus to hippie uprisings. One source concludes regarding Marcuse, "(I)n the 1960s and the

1970s he became known as the preeminent theorist of the New Left and the student movements of West Germany, France, and the United States; some consider him the 'father of the New Left.'"[29]

The ideology embraced by the hippie movement and which now dominates contemporary American culture might best be described using the term "subjectivism." This book uses that term to refer to this ideology. Miriam Webster defines subjectivism as: "1a: a theory that limits knowledge to subjective experience; b: a theory that stresses the subjective elements in experience; 2a: a doctrine that the supreme good is the realization of a subjective experience or feeling (as pleasure); b: a doctrine that individual feeling or apprehension is the ultimate criterion of the good and the right."[30] In other words, subjectivism identifies feelings, subjectivity, as the ultimate measure of reality and therefore the ultimate basis for determining values and making decisions. All these definitions and their collective focus on subjective experience describe the hippie ideology and the culture it spawned.

Foundational Concepts

Three concepts shaped the subjective ideology of the hippie movement.

Live Based on Feelings

The hippie mantra, "If it feels good, do it," embodies the foundational tenet of subjectivism. It sanctioned viewing and responding to life on a subjective basis. Norman Mailer, who significantly influenced the hippie movement, in his essay "The White Negro," published in 1959, refers to the "Hip" person, from which came the term "hippie." He characterized the hip individual as a rebellious white person with "a black man's code," hence the "White Negro."[31]

Mailer described the Hipster's approach to life as having:

> ...almost no interest in viewing human
> nature, or better, in judging human nature, from

a set of standards conceived a priori to the experience, standards inherited from the past. Since Hip sees every answer as posing immediately a new alternative, a new question, its emphasis is on complexity rather than simplicity.... Given its emphasis on complexity, Hip abdicates from any conventional moral responsibility because it would argue that the results of our actions are unforeseeable, and so we cannot know if we do good or bad....[32]

Mailer was asserting that life is too complex to approach it objectively and too unstable to establish a moral code. Therefore, doing what feels good embodies the only moral principle. This perspective provides a formula for unmitigated selfishness. Human feelings, though sometimes kind, notoriously tend toward selfishness. Disconnecting them from any moral constraints results in a proliferation of selfishness. Events such as Woodstock revealed that the only moral consideration resided in maximizing feelings. Consequences such as the trashing of Max Yasgur's farm were of no concern. Identifying feelings as the basis for perceiving reality and making choices licensed unbridled selfishness.

Mailer contended that the universe consists of:

... a changing reality whose laws are remade at each instant by everything living, but most particularly man, man raised to a neo-medieval summit where the truth is not what one has felt yesterday or what one expects to feel tomorrow but rather truth is no more or no less than what one feels at each instant in the perpetual climax of the present.[33]

This pronouncement by Mailer identifies truth with feeling. Since we all experience different feelings that change frequently, truth differs for each of us and is in constant flux. A person goes to sleep in one world and wakes up to a completely new reality. His understanding of the world when he went to sleep does not apply to the world he experiences when he wakes up. This unstable universe eliminates objective knowledge and moral principles, leaving subjective experience as the only valid basis for viewing life and making decisions. In the absence of any structure or morality, the only reasonable choice is to maximize good feelings.

I counseled a woman who had been living with a man but moved out because he had consistently taken advantage of her. During our session, she listed numerous destructive aspects of this relationship that made any thought of her returning irrational. During the next session, she shared with me that she had listened to a song that week that urged her to "follow her heart." She felt her heart telling her to move back with him, and so she did. This woman's rejection of objective realities and her adoption of a subjective decision-making process vividly reflects the ideology of subjectivism and demonstrates its influence on contemporary American society.

This orientation manifests itself in many ways in our current society. For example, commercials tend to lack factual content, instead selling products based on emotions. One automobile commercial shows a family having a good time riding to various places across the country. This commercial provides no objective reasons for buying this car—fuel efficiency, safety ratings, J. D. Power reports. It sold the car based solely on the good feelings depicted in the commercial.

This feelings orientation shows itself in the transgender issue. A person's feelings regarding his gender rather than objective facts related to biological makeup determine reality, even to the extent of giving a biological male who feels like a female entrée into girls' bathrooms and shower rooms.

Identifying feelings as the basis for guiding our lives represents a serious error since, as we observed earlier, God did not design human beings to use their feelings, but their mind and will, as their GPS. Functioning based on our subjective nature results in subhuman existence destined to produce disaster.

Subjective guidance also inhibits agape production. Earlier we saw that optimizing agape requires engagement of our minds and wills. Though sometimes our feelings guide us toward behaviors that benefit others, usually they incline us toward selfishness. Consequently, the subjectivist approach to life guided by feelings is largely devoid of agape. Since agape production supports human and societal health and success, this approach to life leads to precipitous decline.

The Individual Comprises the Only Authority

The hippie cliché, "You have a right to do your own thing," expresses the second tenet of the hippie philosophy. This concept nullifies all external authority, assigning full autonomy to the individual. The term autonomy comes from two Greek words meaning law and self. The autonomous individual is a law unto himself. This precisely describes the hippie perspective. The state, the police, the university, the military, parents, and even God have no right to impose their will on the individual. Hippies conveyed this attitude by referring to police as "pigs." Those on the left still display contempt for law enforcement as manifested in its current initiative to defund police, another reflection of the dominating influence of the hippie movement on contemporary society. The right to do one's own thing constitutes a license for selfishness.

Giving the individual total authority would not be as devastating if he were making decisions based on reason. Employment of his mind and will in the exercise of autonomy would provide guardrails for his choices. Autonomy coupled with the commitment to live according to feelings, the outcome of the first principle cited above, removes those guardrails, resulting in a recipe for disaster. It is like the driver of a car pushing the gas pedal all the way down while taking his hands off the steering wheel. This feelings-driven autonomy constitutes a formula for disaster.

The basis for this authority, the right to do one's thing, resides in the first principle, that of living based on feelings.

Since subjectivism determines reality by feelings, and since I can only feel my own feelings, I am the only real person. All others are merely objects I experience on the monitor of my mind. Since my only interest is enhancing my feelings, the only value of those objects resides in their capacity to make me feel good. Although few sane people would proclaim themselves to be the only real person, in our society this perspective shapes attitudes and values that lead to actions.

Barbara Defoe Whitehead exposes our cultural commitment to this perspective in her book *The Divorce Culture*. Whitehead observes:

> (T)he notion of divorce as the working out of an inner life experience casts it in far more individualistic terms than in the past. Because divorce originated in an inner sense of dissatisfaction, it acknowledged no other stakeholders. Leaving a marriage was a personal decision, prompted by a set of needs and feelings that were not subject to external interest or claims. Expressive divorce reduced the number of legitimate stakeholders in divorce to one, the individual adult.[34]

Here the view that the experiencing individual constitutes the only real person expresses itself in one of life's most significant issues.

Some might assume that subjectivism limits autonomy if one's actions inflict harm on others. However, nothing in the subjectivist theory endorses that position. The individual possesses a right to do his own thing regardless of the impact on others. This unlimited autonomy manifests itself in practices such as abortion, which assigns to the individual the right to kill a baby that is not contributing to one's immediate gratification. Likewise, the right of a transgender biological male to enter a women's shower room trumps the modesty, fears, and safety of women.

Though being the only real person may seem like a great arrangement, it eliminates genuine relationships, thus consigning the individual to a life of solitary confinement. It is not difficult to find a logical connection between the loneliness of seeing oneself as the only real person and the current escalation of the suicide rate.

Even a physically intimate marriage offers no genuine intimacy when one does not assign personhood to his or her spouse. Intimacy can be dangerous because, as Whitehead observed, one's spouse senses no obligation to remain in the relationship if his feelings direct him elsewhere. The individual's view of himself as the only real person has prompted the escalation of cohabitation, a non-committal relationship that limits vulnerability.

Make Choices Based on Immediate Gratification

Another hippie slogan, "Do it now," captures the third tenet of subjectivism. The first principle calls us to live based on feelings. The fact that we can only feel the feelings of the present moment leads to decision-making based on immediate gratification. This perspective nullifies yesterday's commitments and rejects concerns for the future. Recall Mailer's assertion above that "...truth is no more or no less than what one feels at each instant in the perpetual climax of the present." The second principle, the individual has the right to do his own thing, frees him to engage in any form of immediate gratification, regardless of its outcome and impact on others.

Psychedelic drugs constituted a significant aspect of the hippie movement. Their use makes no rational sense. However, if we employ immediate gratification as the basis for decision-making, doing drugs becomes an optimal choice. The current legalizing of drugs in some states reveals our continued embrace and application of this subjective ideology with its emphasis on immediate gratification.

Immediate gratification, doing what feels good now, almost invariably leads to selfish choices. Drugs, overeating, angry responses, sexual promiscuity, and irresponsible purchases all reflect the selfishness of immediate gratification.

Feeling Our Way

Because of subjectivism's feelings orientation, Americans do not hold its tenets at a conscious, rational level but rather at a subjective, attitudinal level. Academics refer to the period since the 1960s as a "post-Christian era," identifying our current culture by what it no longer is rather than by what it is now. Identifying our current culture by what it is not makes little sense. However, our society is compelled to do so for three reasons.

First, most people are unable to objectively identify the beliefs comprising our current ideology. Communists can identify their beliefs, as can socialists, Muslims, and Hindus. But contemporary secular Americans cannot verbalize their core cultural principles. If asked, they usually respond with a litany of unrelated clichés that sound like they are reading from the walls of a serendipity shop. They recite mantras such as, "I believe that everything happens for a purpose," without having given thought to who makes everything happen for a purpose or why they believe it.

A second reason for not identifying the tenets of our current culture in objective terms is that they make no objective sense. Imagine asserting to your boss or spouse that you have a right to do your own thing and plan to do what feels good whenever the feeling arises and have a right to do so because you are the only real person.

This leads us to the third reason for those in our society refraining from objectively expressing the beliefs of subjectivist ideology. They are so blatantly selfish that expressing them comprises admission to embracing selfishness as a way of life. Though our culture gives license to selfishness, human beings nonetheless possess an innate awareness that selfishness does not comprise an admirable trait.

Subjectivism in the Real World

Subjectivism might work to a limited degree for a limited time for unmarried college students in relatively good health, supported by their parents, and living in a safe country that provides a wide array of social services. However, even hippies sheltered from reality by this bubble found life quickly unraveling. Larry Eskridge's description of the devolving scene in Haight-Ashbury during the Summer of Love provides a grim description of that situation.

> The free and easy hippie celebration of sexuality also manifested itself in all sorts of unforeseen "bummers." Venereal diseases were rampant in the Haight, and hippies seeking treatment for syphilis, gonorrhea, and herpes combined with drug overdoses [served] to overwhelm the Free Clinic and the city's health department. Even more troubling was the generally degrading effect life in the Haight had on the young runaway girls who came to the Bay area. As one young teenage girl named Alice told early Jesus People figure David Hoyt, "Girls didn't have any trouble finding a place to spend the night" if they were willing to pay the right price. Others turned to full-fledged prostitution to feed themselves and their drug habits. Sexual violence toward women was also a grim reality. As early as April 1967, one hippie broadside lamented the situation: "Rape is as common as bullshit on Haight Street." In general, by midsummer 1967, women in the Haight were at risk for all sorts of emotional and physical violence from their male counterparts.

> While these discomforts and hardships were daunting enough, the hippies' fervent belief in the spiritual and personal blessings of

drug use was responsible for perhaps the largest share of trouble. Besides growing harassment from the police, overdoses, bad trips, and the hyper-aggressiveness associated with speed were a constant of life in the Haight. These problems multiplied as overcrowding grew and the drug supply's safety and quality were increasingly compromised. A closely related problem was a dramatic increase in assaults and robbery (rip-offs) in the hippie district as a new attempt to control its hitherto free-and-easy drug trade overwhelmed the Golden Rule ethos of the counterculture. As one author described it, "The flower movement was like a valley of thousands of plump white rabbits surrounded by wounded coyotes." When two popular hippie drug dealers were found brutally murdered in separate incidents late that summer, it became clear to many that the bloom was off the hippie rose.[35]

Selfishness produces nothing and destroys everything. This outcome is on full display in the description of life in the Haight-Ashbury district described above. No doubt the destructive nature of unbridled selfishness contributed to the brief, five-year duration of the hippie movement. Individual, relational, and societal health require agape production. Subjectivism promotes full-orbit selfishness. Consequently, it imposes a destructive influence that no society can long endure.

The ongoing influence of this ideology in shaping our current culture is producing similar disastrous results. As of this writing, riots, unbridled destruction, and chaos reflect the influence of the hippie ideology and the emergence of a Haight Ashbury culture on a national scale. The next chapter examines some of the outcomes of subjectivism and the selfishness it produces.

Chapter 3: Agape-Destroying Culture

Trading Agape for Selfishness

Giving the individual the right to do his own thing assigns virtue to selfishness. Subjectivism asserts that doing what I feel like doing comprises the ultimate moral choice and authentic living. Consequently, we now find people announcing proudly, "I did this just for me," as if such behavior displays the epitome of morality, which in fact it does when viewed through the lens of subjectivism.

The anti-authoritarian dimension of subjectivism also promotes selfishness. In most cases, responsiveness to authority promotes the common good, an expression of agape. Living according to civil laws and school rules usually makes for a better society and an environment more conducive to learning, outcomes which benefit others. When children respond to parental authority the family enjoys peace and order. Rejection of authority results in selfishness and chaos.

Likewise, immediate gratification in practically every case guides the individual toward selfishness. Usually the desires of the individual for immediate gratification conflict with the welfare of others. A person may feel like doing drugs for the immediate pleasure they provide. However, doing so will sap his productivity and waste his resources. It may lead to stealing from others. It may also impair his capacity to drive, endangering the lives of others. Immediate gratification seldom produces agape.

Since agape brings success to a society, the selfishness-producing nature of subjectivism not only fails to promote societal welfare but accelerates societal decline.

Even worse, by making the experiencing person the only person, subjectivism eliminates the possibility of agape altogether. Agape entails benefitting others. Subjectivism leaves no other real person to benefit.

Expressions of Selfish Living

Whitehead reports that beginning in the 1960s, selfishness as a virtue became the dominating element of our society's view on divorce:

> People began to judge the strength and "health" of family bonds according to their capacity to promote individual fulfillment and personal growth.... Once the domain of the obligated self, the family was increasingly viewed as yet another domain for the expression of the unfettered self.... Once regarded mainly as a social, legal, and family event in which there were other stakeholders, divorce now became an event closely linked to the pursuit of individual satisfactions, opportunities, and growth.[36]

Whitehead concludes that all obligation to others has been replaced by obligation solely to one's self.

> (O)ne's first obligation in the dissolution of marriage was to oneself.... If expressive divorce excluded the idea that there are other parties at interest in the "divorce experience," it also

overturned earlier notions about one's moral responsibilities to others. An individual's right to divorce was rooted in the individual's right to have a satisfying inner life to fulfill his/her needs and desires. The entitlement to divorce was based on the individual entitlement to pursue inner happiness.... No one, including the divorcing individual's children, had a "right" to intervene in this intensely private experience or to try to disrupt the course of an emotionally healthy journey toward divorce. Nor were there morally compelling arguments for considering the interests and claims of others in the marriage. If divorce was an entirely subjective and individual experience, rooted in a particular set of needs, values, and preferences, then there was no basis for making judgments about the decision to divorce. The new ethic of divorce was morally relativistic: There could be no right or wrong reasons for divorce.... If the divorce experience was an inner journey of the sovereign self, what right had anyone to place impediments in the way?[37]

Framing selfishness as a virtue renders subjectivism's definition of character antithetical to the traditional one. Historically, character consisted of subordinating one's self-interest to those of spouse, children, neighbor, and country. "America the Beautiful" extols those who "more than self their country loved...." These thoughts are foreign to the mind-set of contemporary society, which considers acting selfishly to be noble. Whitehead notes that the core principle underlying Emily Post's well-known book on etiquette was the obligation of the individual "... to please others, to place the comfort and interests of others above one's own."[38] Now such chivalry is not only dead, but we consider it to be wrong.

Subjectivism also devours agape by encouraging people to be takers and not givers. Those in the Haight-Ashbury district during the Summer of Love contracting diseases from promiscuous sex and drugs sought help from the government health facility, that is, they used taxpayer money to support their selfish behavior. This same subjectivist inclination manifests itself in the current popularity of socialism, which demands for oneself what others have earned.

If we evaluate a marriage relationship in terms of a bank account, viewing acts of agape as deposits and acts of selfishness as withdrawals, subjectivism quickly puts a marriage relationship into bankruptcy, producing little agape while manufacturing large quantities of selfishness. Likewise, selfish politicians are bankrupting our nation through self-serving choices.

Subjectivism's Impact on Morality and Grace

We noted that agape consists of two primary components: morality, its foundational expression, and grace, its ultimate expression. Subjectivism undermines both.

The Demise of Morality

Morality consists of giving others what we owe them. Granting the individual the right to do his own thing nullifies all consideration of others, completely eradicating any basis for morality. Also, since the experiencing individual is the only real person, no one else with rights exists. This disregard for the moral rights of others manifests itself in our contemporary subjectivist society.

Our society under the influence of subjectivism does not merely encourage immorality. It has eliminated morality as a category. Cohabitation or the use of pornography are no longer viewed as being immoral. Radio advertisements offer help in avoiding payment of credit card debt. Spenders have no moral obligation to pay for items they purchased.

The Demise of Grace

We defined grace as extending benefits to others that we do not owe them. On this count, subjectivism appears to shine.

Assigning the individual the right to do his own thing with impunity, in effect extends infinite, ongoing grace. Though society owes him nothing, it grants him everything. At first blush, this provision of unlimited, perpetual grace seems to be quite magnanimous. Closer examination, however, exposes it as pseudo-grace on three counts.

First, genuine grace must be granted by another person, whereas the practitioners of subjectivism bestow grace on themselves as manifested in the cliché: "I have a right to do my own thing." This is not grace but rather self-conferred selfishness.

Subjectivist grace is also pseudo-grace because it is granted at the expense of morality. Extending grace to the pregnant woman to deal with her "problem" eliminates any moral obligation to the unborn child. The grace extended to a spouse to walk away from a marriage disregards moral obligations related to marriage and children. Ultimately, granting grace at the expense of morality is selfish because it leads to societal meltdown that hurts everyone.

A third problem with the pseudo-grace of subjectivism resides in the failure of the person extending the grace to pay for it. Earlier we noted that the person extending grace has a moral obligation to pay for it. The person conferring on himself the right to do his thing has a moral obligation to pay the cost of doing so. Subjectivism imposes the costs on others. The right granted a person to do drugs is paid for by society. Society ends up covering the cost of related crime, lack of productivity, and psychological help. Those advocating illegal immigration insist that others cover the costs. Because subjectivism demands that others cover the cost for the grace they extend, this constitutes a form of robbery, a blatant form of selfishness.

Even worse, this pseudo-grace harms the recipient. Empowering the individual to do his own thing without consequences quickly becomes a corrupting force. The human selfishness it unleashes not only harms others but imposes its debasing influence on the perpetrator.

Consequently, subjectivism constitutes pseudo-grace and even anti-grace, an arrangement that consumes agape and promotes selfishness.

Subjectivism Undermines the Agape-Producing Process

Agape requires the employment of our mind and volition. Subjectivism deactivates the intellect and will, replacing them with the emotions as the basis for decision-making.

Suppressing the Mind

Because subjectivism replaces the mind with the emotions as the decision-making tool, our educational system no longer places primary value on factual content and rational skills. Universities issue trigger warnings and safe places to protect the emotions of students from opposing opinions, giving good feelings precedence over factual content and rational analysis.

We hear much about "low-information voters," people who lack sufficient knowledge to make intelligent choices. Our subjectivist-dominated educational system has produced this outcome. Even worse, the subjectivist devaluing of reason and the resulting lack of rational development in our educational system has left many voters lacking the rational skills needed to analyze the meager information they do possess.

Because agape production requires the employment of the mind, underdeveloped intellectual capacities inhibit its production. Our society manifests this outcome in its failure to deal with topics such as abortion, drugs, and sexual identity from a factual and rational perspective.

Disengagement of the mind gives license to the individual to make selfish choices. If I am not confronted by facts and rational analysis related to my choices, I am free to do whatever I please, whatever feels good. Facts related to law enforcement in the United States reveal that racism among police is not endemic. Freed from the responsibility to process such facts, rioters are given license to destroy the livelihood of others.

Disconnecting the Will

Directing our lives by our emotions leaves no role for the will since doing what one feels like doing requires no exercise of volition. Swimming upstream against the current of our desires demands that we exercise our will, but floating downstream with the flow of our feelings does not. Consequently, subjectivism robs the will of exercise, resulting in a lack of selfdiscipline and character. This volitional atrophy shows itself in trends such as irresponsible spending and obesity. Subjectivism, granting the individual the right to do his thing, also discourages discipline in the home and school, previously venues for developing the will and character.

This deficiency in volitional development makes its greatest impact on affluent societies. In developing countries, the challenges of life such as carrying water, chopping wood, and performing other laborious tasks in order to survive develop self-discipline. Instead of chopping wood to keep warm, most Americans need only to touch a thermostat. This absence of discipline-developing demands for survival coupled with the permissiveness engendered by subjectivism is resulting in the underdevelopment of volitional muscle in American society.

This weakness of will undermines agape production. It leaves individuals confronted by difficult agape-producing challenges more likely to opt for easier selfish ones.

Society Devoid of Agape

What practical effects are resulting from subjectivism's selfishness-inducing culture?

The Demise of Virtue

Previously we noted that agape encompasses all other virtues. Consequently, by encouraging selfishness, subjectivism erodes virtues and promotes the corresponding vices. As already noted, subjectivism has engendered a drastic decline of fidelity in marriage and fidelty of politicians to their constituencies.

Demise of Responsibility

Fyodor Dostoevsky stated in *The Brothers Karamazov*, "If God does not exist, everything is permitted."[39] Permitting everything leaves the world in moral chaos.

The other half of this truth, however, is equally as devastating: If God does not exist, nothing is required, i.e., it eliminates responsibility. Granting the individual the right to do his thing exempts him from responsibility. We produce agape both by refraining from evil and meeting our responsibility to do good. By permitting everything and requiring nothing, subjectivism kills agape with a two-edged sword.

Subjectivism has undermined the American sense of responsibility. If you bought a house beyond your means, you are not responsible. It is the bank's fault for lending you the money, and therefore the bank should bear the responsibility. If you bore multiple babies out of wedlock, you should not have to bear responsibility for supporting them. The government should. This abdication of responsibility also shows itself in trends such as grade inflation, which no longer holds students responsible for doing their work.

Perpetual Adolescence

Children are driven by emotions while maturity requires managing our lives with our mind and will. Maturity also requires growing out of adolescent self-centeredness and into adult consideration for others (agape). In replacing agape with selfishness, subjectivism promotes perpetual adolescence, which prevents people from successfully fulfilling adult societal roles.

In her book *The Death of the Grown-Up*, Diana West documents our societal tendency to get stuck in immaturity.

> More adults, ages 18 to 49, watch the Cartoon Network than watch CNN. Readers as old as 25 are buying "young adult" fiction written expressly for teens. The average video gamester was 18 in 1990; now he's going on 30. And no wonder: The National Academy of Science has, in

2002, redefined adolescence as the period extending from the onset of puberty, around 12, to age 30. The MacArthur Foundation has gone further still, funding a major research project that argues that the "transition to adulthood" doesn't end until age 34.... (O)ne-third of the 56 million Americans sitting down to watch SpongeBob SquarePants on Nickelodeon each month in 2002 were between the ages of 18 and 49.[40]

Tying the perpetuation of adolescence to the decline in agape, West observes:

> What has also disappeared is an appreciation for what goes along with maturity: forbearance and honor, patience and responsibility, perspective and wisdom, sobriety, decorum, and manners —and the wisdom to know what is "appropriate," and when.[41]

How could it be otherwise? What else could a culture that discourages the development of the mind and will and advocates the pursuit of doing what feels good produce?

Inhumanity

Perhaps the worst outcome of subjectivism resides in its fostering of inhumanity—attitudes devoid of human sympathies—and the resulting inhumane behaviors. Viewing the experiencing individual as the only real human being eradicates empathy toward others.

This desensitization of human sympathies reveals itself in the growing trend toward mass shootings, abortion, and divorce, where little consideration is manifested toward the pain inflicted on others. Although selfishness and inhumanity have always been present in society, a culture that fosters these darker characteristics of human nature elevates their quantities to unsustainable levels.

The most tragic dimension of American inhumanity resides not in the cruelty it inflicts on others, but rather in the inhumane nature subjectivism breeds in perpetrators. Experiencing inhumanity is terrible; being inhumane is worse.

Reasons for Embracing the Irrational

Since feelings serve as the worst possible GPS for life, why does American society embrace subjectivism?

Cultural AIDS

As the Baby boomer generation reached adulthood, subjectivism went mainstream, becoming the dominant force in our culture—the status it holds today. In the face of so much evidence indicating its destructiveness, why does our society continues to cling to this culture?

We have observed that subjectivism rejects a rational approach to life, instead telling us to follow our feelings. The AIDS virus destroys the defense mechanism of the body, allowing it to continue its destructive work. Likewise, subjectivism by establishing feelings as the basis for determining reality disarms reason, our God-given defense mechanism. By deactivating our rational defenses, subjectivism protects itself against detection as a destructive social virus. This self-protective mechanism has resulted in our society allowing it to continue its destructive work. In other words, subjectivism constitutes cultural AIDS.

The Subjectivist Faith

Subjectivist hope is rooted not in reason but in faith. This faith finds its roots in the belief that authority warps the human personality while autonomy, the right to do one's own thing, produces healthy, responsible human beings. Mailer conveys this faith in the autonomous human being as follows:

> . . . (T)he nihilism of Hip proposes as its final tendency that every social restraint and category be removed, and the affirmation implicit in the proposal is that man would then prove to be more creative than murderous and so would not destroy

> himself. Which is exactly what separates Hip from the authoritarian philosophies which now appeal to the conservative and liberal temper—what haunts the middle of the twentieth century is that faith in man has been lost, and the appeal of authority has been that it would restrain us from ourselves. 42

Adopting this theory requires faith because substantial evidence tells us that it is invalid. Our observation of life reveals that autonomy does not lead to productivity and order. Instead, it produces the chaos displayed at Haight-Ashbury, Woodstock, Occupy Wall Street, and the more recent Capitol Hill Organized Protest (CHOP) in Seattle, in which autonomy has been given free rein. CHOP has even declared itself to be an autonomous nation. Progressive education, which proceeds under the assumption that the autonomous child will behave well and learn much, has been an unmitigated flop. It would only be surprising if it were otherwise. Imagine telling a seasoned teacher that unruly behaviors stem from too much authority and removing all restraint from students would result in their acting responsibly and advancing their education.

History reveals that total autonomy does not produce saints but selfishness. William Bennett catalogs the evidence of this outcome:

> America is the greatest nation in the history of the world—the richest, most powerful, most envied, most consequential. And yet America is the same nation that leads the industrialized world in rates of murder, violent crime, imprisonment, divorce, abortion, sexually transmitted diseases, single-parent households, teen suicide, cocaine consumption, and pornography production and consumption.[43]

Mailer personally displayed the chaotic influence of subjectivism by marrying six times and stabbing his second wife twice with a penknife.[44] The subjectivist faith turns out to be a leap in the dark with every expectation for a destructive landing.

Choosing Who Gets to Do Their Thing

During subjectivism's early years, it preached the message that people have a right to do their own thing. Back in those days, we found Jesus People asserting that their thing was Jesus, and that was okay. They had a right to do their thing, too. I was attending NYU at the time, and I experienced the same openness to my embrace of biblical Christianity from the faculty and other students, even though few shared my position.

Since then the left-wing purveyors of this philosophy have gained power. Now they have changed the rules. Only they have the right to do their thing. Those who disagree must knuckle under. If your thing is cohabitation or homosexuality, that's okay. If your thing is killing a baby that has been conceived as a result of sexual promiscuity, that is okay also. If your thing is to adhere to traditional biblical principles, however, that is not okay. Conservative speakers invited to college campuses should be uninvited or shouted down. The free-speech advocates have morphed into the political correctness tyrants. Though the left has not yet succeeded in totally subjugating Christians, our subjectivist society has advanced substantially in that direction. For example, during the current COVID-19 pandemic, rioters have been extended freedom to congregate while churchgoers have been banned from doing so.

This arrangement is producing the worst of all possible worlds: empowering people driven by selfish desires to do their thing while denying the same freedom to those desiring to promote agape.

Surviving subjectivism

If subjectivism and the resulting selfishness is so destructive, how are we managing to survive? Two factors are temporarily propping up America.

Parasitic Existence

America has survived subjectivism because it took over a society with the greatest store of resources of any nation in history. That included a wealthy economy, a well-developed infrastructure, a substantial manufacturing base, a great educational system, the world's best healthcare system, the world's most powerful military, an effective governmental structure, and many other valuable assets. Our Christian cultural roots also provided a vast supply of human capital: people who were moral, well-educated, living in stable family situations, hard-working, responsible, knowledgeable, skilled, and disciplined. Above all else, like an airplane that has run out of fuel, America had sufficient Christian cultural momentum to forestall a crash landing for an extended time.

Subjectivism, however, has now devoured most of these resources and begun borrowing against projected future production. The Trump presidency, as with Reagan before it, has temporarily stopped the bleeding. However, after the economic success of the Reagan years, progressives regained control and in short order consumed the benefits resulting from his presidency and instigated further decline. We have every reason to believe that a similar outcome will occur after the Trump years. The continued consumption of American capital not only includes economic decline but also the erosion of the family structure, our educational system, and other resources.

Even worse, subjectivism has killed our Christian culture that offered a basis for recovery in the past. A population committed to responsibility, hard work, honesty, courage, fidelity, stable families, and other agape-producing elements provided the necessary human capital to fight our way back. Now we find that both the Christian culture and the human capital it produced have been substantially diminished.

America is like Sampson after his hair was cut, self-deluded into thinking that he still had his previous strength.

Subjectivism continues its parasitic existence by devouring its dying host. On its present course, America will certainly die.

America's only hope lies in the restoration of its past Christian culture.

Cultural Bipolar Disorder

As noted earlier, a subjectivist approach to life, functioning based on feelings rather than reason and volition, quickly leads to disaster. To escape this outcome, America has adopted a bipolar approach to life. It embraces a manic subjectivist ideology to the greatest extent possible. However, when forced by reality, it retreats to what it considers the depressive Christian cultural characteristics of rationality, responsibility, and a semblance of morality.

We witness this inclination in America's election of subjectivist-oriented presidents as long as resources hold out and life does not become too chaotic. However, when our nation begins to experience the economic chaos produced by Pres. Carter, it opts for a return to the financial stability provided by a President Reagan. Or when it encounters the chaos produced by governmental initiatives such as ObamaCare, it gravitates toward a more rational Trump administration. Likewise, a person undergoing brain surgery wants the surgeon to employ mind and will rather than feelings, especially if he may feel like taking off to play 18 holes of golf in the middle of the procedure.

These factors notwithstanding, the priority given to feelings is sufficient to erode our societal well-being. It requires very little manic living to create substantial chaos.

But isn't this bipolar formula—pursuing all the good feelings possible and exercising rational thinking and discipline only when necessary—the way people have always functioned regardless of their culture? Have people not always gone to work because they had to and gone on vacation whenever they could? This is a valid question since this superficial analysis makes our contemporary inclinations seem no different from those of Americans prior to the 1960s.

This assessment fails to recognize the shift in American values since the 1960s. In our previous Christian cultural environment, people prized virtues such as hard work, responsibility, financial stability, and marital fidelity. My parents' sacrifice for their children provided a graphic display of agape, as did their willingness to stay together, to serve others in various ways, to maintain financial responsibility, to live moral lives, to give, to be good neighbors, and to contribute to the community. These were their goals—the kind of persons they strove to be, and the objectives they achieved in large measure. This was the case with a majority in pre-1960s American society.

Liberals love to mock "Leave it to Beaver" as if that existence were only a made-for-television mirage that never existed in real life and therefore constitutes false advertising for the 1950s. It is necessary for them to revise and distort this piece of history to prevent exposure through comparison of the disaster they have created.

But families filled with love in the full-orbed meaning of that term were the norm prior to the 1960s debacle, even though the creators of our current self-centered society cannot imagine human existence so abounding with decency and kindness, responsibility and discipline, morality and grace, and other manifestations of agape. The agape-deficient culture that the propagators of subjectivism have produced is so far beneath our previous Christian society that they must conclude that such a society could not and did not exist. They are wrong.

Of course, I am not suggesting that people in the pre-1960s era consistently pursued agape and invariably reached this goal. The left enjoys setting up the straw man of perfection and then mocking our previous Christian culture for not achieving it. Though agape was not realized to perfection, it was their goal, and they pursued it earnestly, achieving it in large measure—so much so that Tom Brokaw referred to those of the World War II era as the "greatest generation." Aspiring to produce maximum agape as opposed to the subjectivist goal of maximizing good feelings explains the difference in outcomes between then and now.

Note some of the differences: the absence of drugs vs. widespread drug abuse; fidelity in marriage vs. the immediate gratification offered by cohabitation, extramarital affairs, and no-fault divorce; desire for children vs. voluntary childlessness to enjoy more freedom and fun without them; disciplined spending to achieve financial responsibility vs. four cars, big homes, and maxed-out credit cards; and the list could go on and on.

A Congressional Budget Office report revealed that ObamaCare would result in the loss of the equivalent of 2.5 million full-time jobs. In his article entitled "ObamaCare freeing the job-locked poets?" Jonah Goldberg, reported on the exuberant Democrat attitude toward this job loss:

> Democrats insist this is a boon. Indeed, many are talking about it as an act of liberation (which reminds me of an 11-year-old headline from The Onion: "IBM Emancipates 8,000 Wage Slaves").
>
> House Minority Leader Nancy Pelosi says the CBO report vindicates ObamaCare, because "this was one of the goals. To give people life, a healthy life, liberty to pursue their happiness. And that liberty is to not be job-locked, but to follow their passion."
>
> Pelosi is particularly invested in this view. She's been mocked for years now for her repeated claims that ObamaCare is an entrepreneurial bill because it would let Americans quit their jobs to, among other things, "write poetry."[45]

Americans from our previous Christian culture would have viewed such attitudes emanating from government leaders with utter disbelief.

We are like those people suffering from bipolar disorder who do not take their medication because they enjoy the manic phase too much. Those suffering from bipolar disorder when going through the manic phase seem not to believe that it will ever end—but it does. So it will for America.

This bipolar approach to life is dangerous because it takes very little manic behavior to produce very disastrous consequences. One incident of manic behavior such as trying heroin, telling off the boss, unleashing road rage, or buying a house or boat beyond one's means can destroy an individual's life and that of others. Because life cannot tolerate much mania, America's quest for as much mania as possible is wreaking havoc. In a few decades, our manic subjectivist society has squandered the vast resources Americans amassed by discipline and hard work across centuries. I have made reference to cultural tilt, but subjectivism has tilted our society so severely that we are now in freefall.

Manic living is selfish living. Mania is invariably antithetical to agape production just as an explosion tends not to create useful products. Those suffering from bipolar disorder while living in the manic phase hurt themselves and others, especially those closest to them. The current riots are only the most overt expressions of its destruction. American mania is ruining our nation and countless individual lives. Unless we find and apply a remedy, it will soon destroy us.

This section has described the irrational, feelings-oriented, selfishness-inducing secular ideology that currently dominates American society. We can understand why immature college students, carefree and supported by their parents, would embrace this approach to life. However, we wonder why rational adults would not reject this selfishness-producing ideology. They should have recognized its incapacity to support those shouldering adult responsibilities.

The section ahead identifies a psychological theory that gave Americans reason to believe that this ideology would work in the real world. In fact, this psychological perspective provides reason to believe that the hippie ideology will produce the best of all possible worlds. Even more important for the concerns of this book, this theory serves as the bridge between the subjectivism described in this section and its theological version embraced by evangelicals.

SECTION THREE
PSYCHOLOGY OF SELFISHNESS

In light of our human desire to do our own thing and to do what feels good, it is easy to see the attraction of subjectivism. It constituted an offer Americans, especially college students, could not refuse. As those students grew into adulthood, hippies morphed into yuppies, carrying subjectivism from Haight-Ashbury and Woodstock to suburbia, boardrooms, and ultimately to the White House via the presidency of Bill Clinton and coming to full expression with Barack Obama. Though subjectivism has shed some of its external manifestations, its underlying concepts remain embedded in American values, attitudes, and behaviors.

One would think that as Baby Boomers became adults, they would have realized that subjectivism does not work in the real world. They did not. A psychological theory convinced them that subjectivism not only works in real life but that it produces healthy, successful human beings. This section identifies and analyzes that psychological theory.

Chapter 1: The Psychological Theory Shaping American Culture

How could an intelligent, well-educated American society exchange its rational, successful Christian culture for irrational subjectivism? The psychological theory spawned by Carl Rogers assured them that the subjectivist approach to life, doing what feels good, doing one's own thing, would not end in ruin but success.

Though Rogers does not have the name recognition of Sigmund Freud, many in the field of psychology view him as having greater influence on American culture. Writing in 1985, William Kirk Kilpatrick observed: "Carl Rogers is one of the most important social revolutionaries of our time. He is the father of the human potential movement and is arguably the world's most influential living psychologist."[46]

Rogers was born in 1902 in a suburb of Chicago. He attended Union Theological Seminary to train for the ministry but transferred to Columbia University where he earned a Ph.D. in psychology. He taught at Ohio State University, set up a counseling center at the University of Chicago, taught at the University of Wisconsin, and finally accepted a research position at a think tank in La Jolla, California, where he remained until his death in 1987.

Rogers' Personality Theory

Rogers asserted that all life, including human life, possesses a "self-actualizing tendency," a subjective GPS that impels it toward optimal development and behavior. Picture the acorn pushing its way through a crack in the sidewalk to grow into an oak.

Animals following their self-actualizing tendencies, their instincts, seem to be well-adjusted and stress-free. We do not find depressed or schizophrenic squirrels or armies of deer seeking to destroy one another. Why are they emotionally, behaviorally, and relationally healthier than humans?

Rogers contended that humans do not experience the same psychological health because they possess a compelling need for acceptance by significant others—those with whom they have meaningful relationships. If significant others grant that acceptance conditionally, the individual will be able to accept himself only if he meets their conditions of acceptance, standards of performance. "I can only feel good about me if I live up to my parents' expectations."

Therefore, the individual, rather than being guided by his self-actualizing tendency, will be directed by the conditions of acceptance conveyed by significant others. This will produce negative emotional, behavioral, and relational outcomes. Consequently, humans fail to enjoy the tranquility and optimal functioning experienced by animals because they do not follow their self-actualizing tendency but instead are guided by the conditions of acceptance conveyed by significant others.

However, if significant others convey unconditional acceptance, I accept you regardless of your performance, the individual will be able to accept himself unconditionally, without the need to perform in a certain way. Being accepted regardless of his behavior will free him to follow his self-actualizing tendency, which will guide and motivate him to develop a healthy and productive personality and lifestyle.

In his early teens, Bob reflected his mother's personality. She was a cerebral-type person who enjoyed intellectual pursuits. Consequently, Bob's self-actualizing tendency steered him toward academic activities. However, Bob's father was a star athlete in high school. He conveyed that he would accept Bob only if he did the same. Though Bob lacked athletic ability and interests, his need for his father's acceptance compelled him to meet his father's condition of acceptance, i.e. excel at football. Because this was not his natural inclination, the direction his self-actualization would have guided him, he was unsuccessful and unhappy, an outcome that led to depression, relational failures, and ultimately a drug problem.

Bob needed unconditional acceptance from his father. "Bob, it is obvious that you do not possess my athletic inclinations but prefer intellectual pursuits like your mother. I will be proud of you regardless of what direction you take in life." That unconditional acceptance would have enabled Bob to accept himself unconditionally, freeing him to follow his self-actualizing tendency, which would have led him toward academic pursuits, resulting in success and happiness, perhaps becoming the next Elon Musk.

This scenario seems merely to reflect common sense. Of course, Bob's father should not try to force him to be someone he is not. Of course, he should allow his son to follow his academic interests and be proud of him for doing so. Of course, he will be more successful and fulfilled following his natural inclinations.

The dark side of Rogers' theory emerges, however, when the full implications of unconditional acceptance come into play.

Unconditional acceptance mandates that the father accept Bob not only if he pursues academics but also if he prefers to party and do drugs. The theory hypothesizes that if the father displays unconditional acceptance even in the face of these negative inclinations, this unconditional acceptance will unleash Bob's self-actualizing tendency, which will impel him toward productive desires and wholesome behaviors.

Rogers concluded that conditional acceptance constitutes the cause of the full range of human problems and that unconditional acceptance provides the solution. I will refer to this theory as Rogerianism. It might be diagrammed as follows:

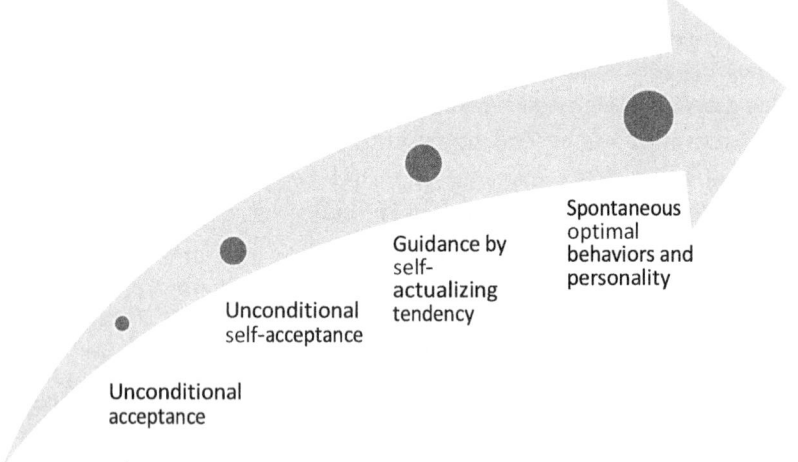

Unconditional self-acceptance

Guidance by self-actualizing tendency

Spontaneous optimal behaviors and personality

Unconditional acceptance

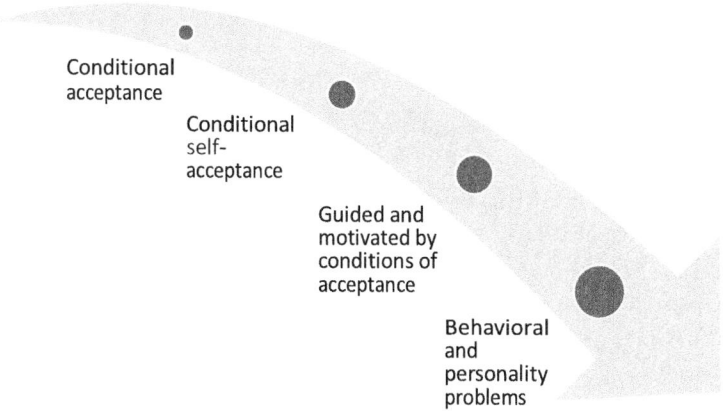

Conditional acceptance

Conditional self-acceptance

Guided and motivated by conditions of acceptance

Behavioral and personality problems

Rogers' Therapeutic Approach

The therapist helps the individual with emotional, behavioral, and relational problems by first developing a relationship in order to become a significant other. As such, he conveys unconditional acceptance to the client. He achieves this by guarding against interjecting his own values or opinions, which might convey conditional acceptance. For example, a question such as, "Bob, do you spend a lot of time partying?" might suggest that Bob needs to be more responsible. To avoid conveying any such judgmental message the therapist merely reflects back the client's own meanings and feelings, an approach labeled non-directive therapy. "So then, Bob, you enjoy having a good time with your friends." The experience of the therapist's unconditional acceptance enables Bob to accept himself unconditionally, that is, to feel good about himself regardless of his attitudes or behaviors. Rogers hypothesized that this experience of unconditional acceptance and the resulting unconditional self-acceptance free Bob to be guided by his self-actualizing tendency, which will prompt him toward healthy development and behaviors.

Applications

Rogers believed this theory could be applied to virtually every type of problem such depression, anxiety, behavioral issues, and relational problems. Consequently, it found application not only in psychotherapeutic settings but in parental, educational, and other venues. Rogers also envisioned that his theory would help healthy people maximize their potential. For example, unconditional self-acceptance could give a major-league batter the confidence needed to increase his batting average. Rogers believed his theory could help groups and society as a whole. Conditional acceptance constitutes the foundational cause of human problems, and unconditional acceptance provides the remedy.

The Dominating Influence of Rogers' Theory

Several powerful factors catapulted Rogers' theory into prominence, which in turn resulted in unconditional acceptance becoming the dominating concept of our culture.

Subjectivism in Psychological Terms

Unconditional acceptance, Rogers' core concept, parallels subjectivism in that it extends to the individual the right to do his own thing. The unconditionally accepted individual has the latitude to behave as he pleases without disapproval or negative consequences. In other words, unconditional acceptance assigns autonomy to the individual. The father who accepts Bob unconditionally has no basis for faulting his drug habit but has in effect granted him the freedom to pursue it.

In addition, both Mailer and Rogers predict that this autonomy will produce positive outcomes. They believe that the individual accepted unconditionally, granted autonomy, will choose the most productive path.

This synergy between subjectivism and Rogers' theory established their joint message of unconditional acceptance as the foundational ideology of American post-Christian culture. A current manifestation of our cultural commitment to unconditional acceptance expresses itself in identity politics and intersectionality, which decry the unwillingness of American society to accept various groups unconditionally and mandates that it does.

Assurance of Support from Science

Rogers and Norman Mailer differ, however, in that Mailer based his confidence in a good outcome on faith in humanity while Rogers claimed support from psychological research, i.e. science. According to Rogers, science assures us that the person freed to do his own thing, to follow his self-actualizing tendency, will develop into a wholesome human being. Therefore, the theory of Carl Rogers constitutes subjectivism, only framed as psychology, which gave it scientific credibility.

Rogers' assurance of scientific support comprised the necessary ingredient for selling subjectivism to American adults. Hippies were happy to claim the right to do their own thing, to do what feels good, based on Mailer's blind faith, even in the face of a tsunami of empirical evidence warning of disastrous results. However, Americans bearing adult responsibilities needed proof that a perpetual Woodstock would somehow be productive. Rogers provided subjectivism with that proof. He claimed scientific evidence for the position that people accepted unconditionally, freed to do their own thing, will become psychologically healthy and productive. Embracing subjectivism no longer required Mailer's leap of faith but, according to the research of a leading psychologist, rested on a scientific foundation.

Irresistible Appeal

Americans also embraced Rogers' theory because of its irresistible appeal. Subjectivism offered the individual the right to do his own thing. Rogers improved on this offer by promising scientific assurance that doing one's thing would optimize the life of the individual and society.

Imagine waking up every morning knowing that you would be—or at least should be—accepted unconditionally that day, i.e. regardless of your attitudes, words, and actions. If others do not accept you unconditionally, they have the problem. Equally appealing is the assurance that accepting yourself unconditionally leads to your becoming your optimized self. A chapter in one of Rogers' major books entitled "To Be That Self Which One Truly Is" gives assurance of this outcome.[47]

Unconditional acceptance also offers freedom from blame and guilt. If I behave in ways some may consider inappropriate, this behavior stems from their failure to accept me unconditionally. Therefore, the fault is theirs and not mine.

The ultimate appeal of unconditional acceptance is that, as with subjectivism, it assigns autonomy to the individual. It frees him to behave as he chooses and allows him to determine his own morality. Whatever his self-actualizing tendency leads him to do is the *right* thing to do. No one has any right to judge his behavior.

Self-Help

Rogers' theory also received wide acceptance because it could be employed on a self-help basis. Freudian therapy required trained psychiatrists, making this cure costly and time-consuming. The Rogerian approach merely required reading a book or attending a seminar and then applying Rogers' principles to one's own life or to children, students, or others. The old warning, "Don't try this at home," did not apply. This led to a flood of self-help books and seminars, each presenting Rogers' approach in its own distinctive way.[48] Perhaps Rogers has not enjoyed the same name recognition as Freud because so many other psychologists, authors, and speakers popularized his theory.

The Solution to Almost Everything

Subjectivism did not promise to fix anything, but seemed only to find application to love-ins and rock concerts—not especially productive activities. By way of contrast, Rogers' theory, as previously noted, promised to solve practically every kind of problem and enhance human development. Later in life, Rogers traveled the globe seeking to apply his theory in the promotion of national and world peace.

Substitute for Christianity

Christianity ensconces love as the ultimate virtue. Rogers viewed love and acceptance as synonymous. Equating love and acceptance linked Rogers' theory with Christianity, both having love and acceptance as a central theme. This connection between Rogerianism and Christianity provides Rogers' theory with a religious aura. As a result, Rogers' theory filled the void for post-Christian Americans who were feeling the absence of a religious dimension. Embracing his theory allowed them to feel that they were being religious, only without the need for church and ritual. In fact, this arrangement allowed them to feel superior, being above the trappings of institutional Christianity, instead focusing on love (unconditional acceptance), the heart of the matter.

In many ways' psychology has replaced Christianity in our society as a secular religion. Psychologists now fill many roles formerly assigned to a pastor or priest. Previously people took their problems to their pastors, while now they seek help from therapists. Conversely, many pastors now counsel and even preach from a psychological perspective. By functioning as a secular religion, Rogers' theory garnered even greater cultural influence.

The Magnanimous Image of Unconditional Acceptance

Rogers' perspectives also appealed because unconditional acceptance and love appears to comprise the ultimate virtue. What could be wrong with a theory promoting unconditional acceptance and love? It would seem that only an evil or misguided person would oppose this concept.

Adoption As Our Cultural Foundation

Rogers' theory has become the dominant force in our culture. As such, it has implanted the cultural message that accepting unconditionally is always beneficial and loving while failing to do so is hurtful and hateful. As a result, our society now values accepting unconditionally as invariably moral while viewing failure to accept unconditionally as immoral. Consequently, unconditional acceptance has become our only but sufficient moral principle and cultural value. Therefore, it has elevated concepts such as tolerance as absolutes in our culture.

Because unconditional acceptance promises to provide the solution to the broad range of human problems and to optimize human potential, American culture has ensconced it as a way of life. With it, life runs well. Without it, when individuals and societies convey conditional acceptance, pathologies result. If we would all just learn to accept one another unconditionally, we would all develop into well-adjusted personalities and our society would become peaceful and productive.

Brendan Eich, the creator of the JavaScript programming language, worked at Mozilla for 15 years and was named CEO in 2014. It was discovered, however, that back in 2008 Eich made a $1,000 contribution in support of Proposition 8 in California, which called for the confining of marriage to one man and one woman. Many in the company viewed this contribution as a failure to accept gays unconditionally, thus violating our culture's compelling moral principle of unconditional acceptance. This resulted in a movement within the company to have him removed as CEO, pressure that ultimately led to his resignation.[49]

One can hardly imagine a more tepid expression of nonacceptance than a $1,000 contribution made six years earlier toward a cause that did not condemn homosexuality but merely circumscribed the definition of marriage. Yet this tiny transgression of our cultural moral code of unconditional acceptance was sufficient to force the outing of a CEO of a major company, despite his very significant previous accomplishments and contributions to the company.

This incident graphically demonstrates our culture's embrace of unconditional acceptance as its dominant moral principle and core cultural value.

The exception to our culture's commitment to unconditional acceptance resides in the non-acceptance of evangelical Christians and conservative Jews because our society views biblical morality as demanding conditions of acceptance, and therefore those committed to biblical values are viewed as a societal cancer.

Identifying Our Post-Christian American Culture

We identify our current culture as post-Christian, indicating that it is no longer Christian but something else. That something else is subjectivism, especially as expressed in the theory of Carl Rogers and its core concept of unconditional acceptance.

This post-Christian culture manifests its presence in countless ways. For example, our news and entertainment media produce content that reflects unconditional acceptance as their guiding principle. Nudity, profanity, fornication, adultery, and homosexuality are all accepted, and anyone unwilling to accept them will be shamed and silenced with labels such as judgmental, close-minded, bigoted, discriminatory, self-righteous, and hater. Our educational institutions promote similar values and attitudes. We find the same influence of unconditional acceptance displayed in government policies with the acceptance of abortion, sanctuary cities, granting welfare benefits virtually unconditionally, and in other policies and practices.

Though exceptions to unconditional acceptance exist, these holdouts are constantly being diminished. For example, even non-acceptance of pedophilia is being eroded through the lowering of the age of consent and assertions by some that sexual relations between adults and children are not harmful to children. In theory, post-Christian culture espouses unconditional acceptance of everything. Our practices keep moving toward that ideal.

The Compelling Question

Rogers claimed scientific support for his theory. Based on that assurance, Americans adopted Rogers' central principle of unconditional acceptance as our core moral concept and a way of life.

Was Rogers correct in his assertion of scientific support? If so, our culture has taken a major step forward by adopting unconditional acceptance. If, however, Rogers' claim is not valid, Americans have made a serious mistake in embracing it. Next, we will examine an experiment that graphically reveals whether America made the right choice.

Chapter 2: The Experiment

The Setting

We can make a compelling assessment of Rogers' theory by looking at the outcome of what may have been his most extensive experiment designed to show its effectiveness. Rogers applied his theory at a Catholic school system in California operated by the Sisters of the Immaculate Heart of Mary (IHM). The school system consisted of 60 schools including a college and was staffed by 560 nuns. Rogers appointed William Coulson, a colleague who had worked closely with him for many years, as project coordinator.

This experiment provided a good test for the effectiveness of Rogers' theory for a number of reasons. It began in 1966 when Rogers was at the prime of his career. He had done therapy for about 35 years, had taught for 23 years, and five years earlier had published perhaps his most significant book, *On Becoming a Person: A Therapist's View of Psychotherapy*. This experiment applied his concepts on a large scale and in various settings such as with individuals, in groups, and with an organization as a whole.[50] In addition, IHM had a strong liberal orientation, which promised a welcoming audience for Rogers' ideas. Beyond that, this experiment took place in Southern California in the late 1960s, a time and place in which subjectivism was flourishing.

This experiment also provided a good assessment of Rogers' ideas because of its dramatic results. As you will see, the findings were *not* ambiguous.

Beginning in 1966, IHM invited Rogers, Coulson, and 58 facilitators to organize encounter groups that included administrators, teachers, and students.[51] These groups provided a non-threatening environment of unconditional acceptance that freed participants to experience and express their feelings, that is, to engage in "non-directive self-exploration."[52]

The Results

The short-term results looked positive. Coulson recalled:

Rogers and I did a tape for Bell and Howell [the project sponsors] summarizing that project; and I talked about some of the short-term effects and said that when people do what they deeply want to do, it isn't immoral.[53]

However, before long the situation deteriorated. Coulson later reflected, "We hadn't waited long enough."[54] He reported that within a year, 300 of the 560 nuns "were petitioning Rome to get out of their vows. They did not want to be under anyone's authority, except the authority of their imperial inner selves."[55]

Coulson cites "a tragic book called *Lesbian Nuns, Breaking Silence*, which documents part of our effect on the IHM and other orders that engaged in similar experiments...."[56] It recounts lesbian activity among nuns resulting from the influence of these groups. Coulson reflects:

An older nun in the group, "freeing herself to be more expressive of who she really was internally," decided that she wanted to make love with Sister Mary Benjamin. Well, Sister Mary Benjamin engaged in this; and then she was stricken with guilt, and wondered, to quote from the book, "Was I doing something wrong, was I doing something terrible? I talked to a priest —."[57]

Coulson explained:

Unfortunately, we had talked to him first. "I talked to the priest," she says, "who refused to pass judgment on my actions. He said it was up to me to decide if they were right or wrong. He opened a door, and I walked through the door, realizing I was on my own."[58]

Coulson also speaks of "seductions in psychotherapy, which became virtually routine in California."[59] Coulson attributed this to the fact that "we had trained people who didn't have Rogers' innate discipline from his own fundamentalist Protestant background, people who thought that being themselves meant unleashing libido."[60]

Coulson cited a book entitled *Hollywood Priest*, which described how one of the nuns from the IHM order "got in the spirit of Rogerian non-directive encounter"[61] and propositioned a priest. Therapists were assigned to nuns who opened up too much in the encounter groups.[62] When the priest refused, the nun became sexually involved with her Rogerian therapist. Coulson reported:

He got her involved in sex games, in therapy. Rogers didn't get people involved in sex games, but he couldn't prevent his followers from doing it, because all he could say was, "Well, I don't do that." Then his followers would say, "Well, of course you don't do that, because you grew up in an earlier era; but we do, and it's marvelous; you have set us free to be ourselves and not carbon copies of you."[63]

This response demonstrates that unconditional acceptance actually does grant the individual the right to do his thing. Here we find therapists becoming sexually involved with clients who are nuns, which constitutes a betrayal of their host institution and a breach of professional ethics. Unconditional acceptance granted these therapists and nuns the moral right to participate in these behaviors.

Coulson recalled: "(W)e called off the study after two years because we were alarmed about the results. We thought we could make the IHM better than they were; and we destroyed them."[64] This project resulted in the closing of all but one of the 60 schools. Of the 560 nuns, Coulson estimated that only a few dozen remained.

These results troubled Rogers, who shared his concerns in an interview Coulson taped in 1976:

> I left there feeling, Well, I started this . . . thing, and look where it's taking us; I don't even know where it's taking me. I don't have any idea what's going to happen next. And I woke up the next morning feeling so depressed that I could hardly stand it. And then I realized what was wrong. Yes, I started this thing, and now look where it's carrying us. Where is this going to carry us? And did I start something that is in some fundamental way mistaken and will lead us off into paths that we will regret?[65]

This upheaval at IHM has been attributed to various causes. In an article in the *Journal of the History of the Behavioral Sciences*, Robert Kugelmann attributes the destructive outcomes to struggles resulting from IHM pushing against Archbishop Cardinal McIntyre's more conservative orientation.[66]

However Coulson, a recognized professional who oversaw the project and was himself a Catholic, was well-positioned to make an accurate analysis. It is doubtful he would assume responsibility for the calamitous results without a good reason for doing so. Likewise, in the interview cited above, Rogers conveys responsibility for the negative results. He probably would not have done so if another plausible cause existed. The fact that he called off the experiment also reveals his sense that it was producing these negative outcomes.

Coulson reported that Rogers performed five additional unsuccessful educational projects.[67] Rogers himself ultimately expressed doubts about his theory. Toward the end of his life while speaking to the Association of Humanistic Psychology, Rogers lamented, "I hope Rogerian therapy goes down the drain ... Yes, you can try to grow to be more often empathic, and more often feel an unconditional regard for this person, but it is not something you should do."[68] Rogers' hope that Rogerian therapy would go down the drain has gone unrealized. Rather, his ideas represent the most dominant force shaping contemporary American culture.

What Went Wrong

If Rogers' theory were correct, what should have resulted from his IHM experiment? The environment of unconditional acceptance should have liberated the participants to follow their self-actualizing tendencies. Through the guidance of their self-actualizing tendencies, participants should have discarded emotional, behavioral, and relational baggage and blossomed into wholesome personalities engaged in productive behaviors and harmonious relationships. Even if these results did not emerge fully, this unconditionally accepting environment should have produced significant progress in these directions, demonstrating that unconditional acceptance frees the self-actualizing tendency to optimize human functioning.

Rogers' experiment produced the opposite results because the two driving principles of Rogers' theory embody two erroneous assumptions: 1) that human beings will function optimally when guided by their self-actualizing tendency; 2) that unconditional acceptance will free the self-actualizing tendency to produce that result. Here are the problems with those concepts.

Guidance by Our Subjective Natures Promotes Selfishness

Rogers' first error resided in his theory regarding the self-actualizing tendency. Rogers was right in his assumption that those in the experiment who received unconditional acceptance would experience the freedom to display their subjective selves. Rogers was wrong, however, in his assessment of the nature of the subjective human component that would be released. He assumed that it consisted of a human self-actualizing tendency that would produce optimal human behavior.

This belief conforms to the typical humanistic template. Those holding humanistic beliefs such as Rogers contend that at the core of the individual is a drive toward goodness just waiting to emerge, but something is suppressing it. Thus, if we can only identify and remove this blockage, human innate goodness will gush out, inundating the individual and society with goodness.

Rogers was convinced that the self-actualizing tendency constituted that positive human inner-drive waiting to be unleashed, and conditional acceptance comprised the barrier preventing its release. Unconditional acceptance would remove this blockage. Unconditional acceptance did in fact free the human subjective inclinations of those in the experiment to express themselves. They discovered, however, that this subjective drive was not a self-actualizing tendency that produced optimal behavior but a depraved nature that inclined the individual toward selfishness and destructive behavior. In other words, scripture is correct in its teaching regarding fallen human nature.

Of all groups, we might expect that the nuns engaged in this experiment when freed to express their subjective inclinations would have displayed agape-oriented responses rather than selfishness. They had chosen a profession requiring self-sacrifice in order to serve others.

Yet, when liberated by unconditional acceptance to follow their subjective inclinations, they did not display an agape-producing self-actualizing tendency but selfishness. Their unbridled sexual inclinations harmed rather than helped others. Likewise, abandoning their orders was hurtful to the Roman Catholic Church, the school system, and its students. These outcomes reveal that even in a community of nuns, freeing human nature to follow its subjective inclinations produces a Summer of Love without drugs, a Woodstock without music, but enough promiscuous sex to compensate.

Unconditional Acceptance Provides a License for Selfishness

A second reason for the dramatic, negative outcome of Rogers' experiment resides in the absolute autonomy granted through unconditional acceptance. Unconditional acceptance, it turns out, comprises a very powerful phenomenon that liberates human beings to live selfishly. People seldom consider the actual meaning of the term unconditional acceptance, probably because it sounds so magnanimous. Its destructive power, however, becomes obvious once we analyze the vastness of its implications.

Taken at face value, unconditional acceptance extends authority to the recipient to behave in any way he chooses without consequence. Unconditionally accepting an individual mandates accepting him when he acts immorally, thus eradicating the moral rights of others. Therefore, it permits the individual to inflict whatever harm he chooses on others. Consequently, accepting an individual unconditionally means that other people do not matter. The unconditionally accepted person's feelings are the only consideration. Accepting the illegal immigrant unconditionally conveys that working Americans burdened with paying for his benefits do not matter, nor does the welfare of citizens more vulnerable to disease and crime. Likewise, allowing transgender biological males into girls' shower rooms makes their unconditional acceptance the only consideration, robbing the girls of their safety and dignity.

Therefore, unconditional acceptance frees the individual to adopt a totally selfish lifestyle.

Why We Need to Take Unconditional Acceptance at Face Value

Some might contend that we should not take the term unconditional acceptance at face value. We must take it at face value, however, for the following reasons:

- First, unconditional acceptance as described above is exactly what the term means. Therefore, when we use the term that is precisely what we are conveying. If the person using it intends a different meaning, he is obligated to use different words.

- Seldom if ever do those employing this term put qualifiers on it, for example saying, "We should accept individuals unconditionally as long as their actions do not hurt other people." This absence of qualifiers indicates that they mean the term to be taken literally.

- Placing qualifiers (conditions) on unconditional acceptance results in it no longer being unconditional, since conditions make acceptance conditional. Consequently, using this term if we intend any conditions is erroneous and misleading.

- The participants and staff in Rogers' experiment displayed a literal understanding of unconditional acceptance in viewing promiscuous behavior as okay. This reveals that those initiating and propagating this concept intended its literal meaning.

- The behaviors now accepted by our society display a literal understanding of unconditional acceptance. For example, we sanction murder in the form of abortion and euthanasia, accept fornication via cohabitation, celebrate homosexuality, and have legalized recreational marijuana.

These factors compel us to take the term unconditional acceptance at face value. As such, it extends to the individual a license to live selfishly.

Accepting the Person but Not His Behavior

Some attempt to avoid the vast negative implications of unconditional acceptance by employing the cliché, "I accept you but not your inappropriate behavior." In other words, if you display inappropriate behavior, I will accept you as a person, but I reserve the right to respond to you at the behavioral level with disapproval, discipline, or some other consequence. This perspective allows parents or other authority figures to deal with *behaviors* they deem to be harmful while still claiming to accept the *person* unconditionally.

This solution does not work for several reasons.

Non-Rogerian

Accepting the person but not his behavior violates Rogers' theory. He would view accepting the person but rejecting his behavior as a breach of unconditional acceptance, as being judgmental, as imposing our values and standards on the other person. We noted previously that Rogers' theory forced him to accept the behaviors of therapists involved sexually with clients. He did not respond by saying, "I think you are a fine person, but I condemn your behavior." His theory does not allow that.

Can you imagine a Rogerian therapist telling a client, "I want you to know that I accept you as a person, but your behaviors are reprehensible"? That would never happen. Therefore, the cliché, "I accept you but not your inappropriate behavior," does not represent Rogers' theory.

The Person and His Behavior are Inseparable

This cliché encounters an even more serious problem in its attempt to separate the person from his behavior. This position conveys that no moral connection exists between persons and their behaviors. This theory conflicts with Jesus' mandate to "Either make the tree good and its fruit good, or make the tree bad and its fruit bad...." (Matthew 12:33)

This separation of persons from behaviors is not possible because a person's behavior flows from and reflects his character, the essence of who he is. Jesus taught:

> "For from within, out of the heart of man, come evil thoughts, sexual immorality, theft, murder, adultery, coveting, wickedness, deceit, sensuality, envy, slander, pride, foolishness. All these evil things come from within, and they defile a person" (Mark 7:21-23).

Behaviors do not appear out of thin air. They come from the heart, the character, the core of the personality. Therefore, the heart and behavior are indissolubly integrated. Consequently, we must either accept the person and his behavior or reject the person and his behavior. We cannot pronounce the person to be acceptable while labeling his behavior as unacceptable.

Eradicating the Significance of Character

Accepting both the selfish person and the one displaying agape conveys that the exercise of sacrifice, responsibility, and discipline by the person of character has no value. The character of the selfish person is as acceptable as that of the person who consistently displays agape.

Imagine that parents have two sons. One studies hard and behaves well while the other is on drugs, disregards schoolwork, and engages in promiscuous sex. These parents, steeped in our core cultural concept of unconditional acceptance, assert that the persons, the characters, of both of their sons are equally acceptable. Doing so conveys that the hard work and discipline of the son displaying character are valueless. This devaluing of character has led to a scarcity of this valuable commodity in American society.

Undermining Discipline

This cliché also discourages disciplining those practicing bad behavior. We discipline persons, not behaviors. If we accept the person, there is no basis for disciplining him. Yet, it is impossible to discipline behaviors. It makes no sense to say, "You don't have to go to your room for timeout, just your behavior has to go." Parents and other authority figures probably do not go through these theoretical gymnastics. However, they nonetheless sense that accepting the person leaves no legitimate basis for disciplining him, even though they may disapprove of his behavior.

In summary, accepting the person but not his behavior fails to resolve the moral dilemma and practical problems created by unconditional acceptance. In the end, unconditional acceptance requires that we accept both the person and his behavior. This tidy cliché resolves nothing. Rather, it is dangerous because many people believe that it does provide a solution to the moral bankruptcy of unconditional acceptance when it does not.

Eradicating Value

Unconditional acceptance proves disastrous in its eradication of the individual's value. The license to live selfishly may seem like a fantastic arrangement to the individual. However, its serious downside resides in its dehumanizing implication. At the very heart of our value as a human being resides the capacity to deploy our mind and will to make consequential choices. Accepting a person regardless of his choices, whether he lives selfishly or produces agape, conveys that his decisions have no value. Asserting that a person's choices do not matter sends the message that his existence has no significance.

This loss of value can lead to a sense of futility, which can engender depression and suicide, both rampant in our society. If we are accepted regardless of our attitudes and behaviors, why do the hard work of confronting life's challenges? Why not live in the fantasy worlds of movies, video games, marijuana, and pornography? Or, why not opt out altogether?

Formula for Character Weakness

Rogers' theory in giving the individual a license to behavior selfishly promotes character weakness. Accepting individuals unconditionally eliminates the need to develop discipline and strength of character. Affirming that they are okay just the way they are allows them to spend their life floating downstream with the current of their desires and never needing to swim upstream against the tide of their feelings. This arrangement produces individuals lacking substance.

Rogers' experiment exposed the potential of unconditional acceptance to inflict incalculable damage. The chapter ahead describes the devastation it is inflicting on our society.

Chapter 3: Societal Destruction

We observed in the previous two chapters that the core component of the theory of Carl Rogers, unconditional love and acceptance, has become the sole moral principle and way of life for contemporary American society. This chapter describes the devastating impact of this cultural orientation.

Destroying Relationships

Rogers' theory is especially destructive to relationships. It spawned the belief that the ultimate relationship consists of people who accept each other unconditionally. In the optimal marriage, the husband and wife display unconditional love and acceptance toward each other. This arrangement presupposes that unconditionally accepted spouses will spontaneously and consistently display loving behavior. This perspective, as with Rogers' experiment, fails to take into account the human inclination toward selfishness. Unconditional acceptance provides spouses with a license to behave selfishly, and they will exercise that prerogative far too frequently to maintain a good marriage.

In reality, conditions comprise an essential ingredient for all relationships, establishing guard rails against selfishness and providing them with meaning, structure, and the basis for functioning. For example, marriage derives its meaning from conditions such as a lifelong commitment, living together, and sexual exclusivity. Granting spouses freedom to have sexual relations with others deprives marriage of its meaning. If a spouse could live wherever he or she chose, a marriage would lose its structure and capacity to function. Whatever we might call the resulting relationship, it would not comprise marriage as we know it.

Every relationship requires conditions to survive and function effectively: employer and employee, citizen and those who govern, friendships, neighbors, extended family, etc. We find embedded within each type of relationship its own unique set of conditions.

Boundaries comprise conditions identifying what a relationship does *not* include. For example, a business relationship does not include the right to intimacy. One neighbor has no right to trespass on the property of another without permission. The current emphasis on boundaries reveals that despite our society's commitment to unconditional acceptance, people instinctively recognize that relationships require conditions.

Establishing and meeting reasonable conditions results in friendly and well-ordered relationships that fulfill their intended purpose and benefit those engaged in them. Without conditions chaos reigns, people are hurt, and relationships disintegrate. We witnessed this outcome in Rogers' experiment.

Because conditions provide relationships with meaning, structure, and the capacity to function, our society's adoption of unconditional acceptance as a core cultural value is producing relational disintegration. Cohabitation is supplanting marriage because unconditional acceptance does not support the more demanding but more rewarding marriage relationship. Without conditions to govern the interaction between parents and children, parents are finding their relationship with their children much less satisfying and therefore opting for fewer children or none at all. Educators look every which way to figure out why our schools are failing. Establishing traditional student/teacher relational conditions would go a long way toward restoring American educational order and proficiency.

Role-Reversal

Most people want to be accepted unconditionally but are not enthusiastic about doing the acceptance. A husband is happy to have his wife accept him even when he is cranky and unreasonable but prefers to reserve the right to object when *she* is cranky and unreasonable.

Consequently, society must designate who extends unconditional acceptance and who receives it. Our culture requires those historically in positions of authority to do the unconditional accepting, while it designates those historically under authority to receive unconditional acceptance. Parents, teachers, therapists, and the like are expected to accept unconditionally whereas children, students, and clients get to receive unconditional acceptance. Apparently, society makes these assignments because groups such as children and students are viewed as weaker and more vulnerable, and therefore we must give their welfare higher priority, which according to Rogers' theory means accepting them unconditionally. Since we tend not to enjoy doing the accepting, those called to accept unconditionally get paid to do so, except for parents. That factor may contribute to parents are having fewer children.

Extending unconditional acceptance to persons grants them the right to do their own thing, which places them in control of the relationship. For example, students accepted unconditionally control the classroom. This arrangement results in role-reversal. Those previously in authority are now under authority and vice versa. Unconditional acceptance empowers children to behave as they wish while parents are responsible for providing support.

Experience tells us that this role-reversal does not work. Children are not qualified to control the home, nor are students capable of effectively guiding the educational process.

Even worse, this role-reversal grants authority to children, students, and others without assigning to them commensurate responsibility. Instead, those previously in authority continue to bear the responsibilities for behaviors and outcomes, even though they had been stripped of the authority necessary to meet those responsibilities. When the home or educational system begin to fail, no one blames the children or students who are now in control. Instead, society continues to hold parents and teachers responsible.

Relationships can work only when authority and responsibility correspond. A person given authority without being assigned the related responsibility tends to abuse that authority. Likewise, assigning responsibility without commensurate authority results in frustration and failure. A teacher told me that she is held responsible for her students' school attendance, though she has no authority to control it.

Their failure to show up results in a reduction in her pay.

The role reversal created by the unconditional acceptance of selected groups has produced a relational structure that is creating havoc in American homes, schools, and other venues.

Sociopathic Society

Unconditional acceptance produces an even more sinister by-product. According to Rogers' theory, the goal of unconditional acceptance is to engender unconditional *self*-acceptance, which he believed would free the person to be guided by his self-actualizing tendency.

Rogers was correct that the unconditionally accepted person tends to develop unconditional self-acceptance. In the absence of conditions and the discipline they invoke, the individual feels good about himself regardless of his behavior. A student never told that his answers are wrong will tend to feel good about his performance as a student. Charles Krauthammer exposed this reality in a 1990

Time Magazine article entitled "Education: Doing bad but feeling good." He wrote:

> A standardized math test was given to 13year-olds in six countries last year. Koreans did the best. Americans did the worst, coming in behind Spain, Britain, Ireland and Canada. Now the bad news. Besides being shown triangles and equations, the kids were shown the statement "I am good at mathematics." Koreans came last in this category. Only 23% answered yes. Americans were No. 1, with an impressive 68% in agreement.[69]

We have no reason to believe that American students were not as intelligent as those of other countries. Apparently, American students were made to feel good about themselves unconditionally, regardless of their level of effort and achievement. This unconditional self-acceptance resulted in their underachieving.

Deactivation of the Conscience

Unconditional self-acceptance by definition entails the deactivation of the conscience. If I feel good about me regardless of how I live, my conscience has ceased to function. Unconditional acceptance produces this outcome by stripping the conscience of any basis for producing guilt.

Guilt can be destructive when invalid, but the conscience and the valid guilt it produces are necessary to keep us functioning humanely. It is good when morality and kindness rather than guilt motivate us to behave humanely. However, none of us behave as we should entirely in response to positive motivations. Most individuals, men especially, drive the speed limit not out of a desire to be model citizens but to avoid flashing blue lights in their rearview mirror.

It is better to have guilt motivating people to do the right thing than to have them do evil. Would we rather have a person not steal from us out of guilt or to steal from us? Therefore, the guilt produced by the conscience plays a major role in maintaining a decent society. A society where no one felt guilt would quickly disintegrate into a world of chaos and cruelty.

Influencing Society toward Sociopathology

The reduction of guilt resulting from the promotion of unconditional self-acceptance has inclined us toward becoming a sociopathic society. A major characteristic of a sociopath is the inclination not to feel guilt even when committing acts that harm others. Sociopathology and psychopathology have been defined as follows:

> Both psychopaths and sociopaths lack a moral compass. They are generally incapable of sympathizing with the feelings of others, and lack the set of ethics that tend to keep society from dissolving into a chaotic mess where everyone only looks out for themselves.[70]

Unfortunately, we see our society trending toward this description under the influence of unconditional self-acceptance.

The terms psychopath and sociopath are often viewed as interchangeable. The fifth edition of the Diagnostic and Statistical Manual of Mental Disorders (DSM-5), released by the American Psychiatric Association in 2013, lists both sociopathy and psychopathy under the heading of Antisocial Personality Disorders (ASPD).[71] Both display the absence of normal guilt feelings. However, there is a distinction. The psychopath is considered to be inclined in this direction by nature while the sociopath has developed this personality trait under the influence of his environment, e.g. a permissive parent.[72]

This distinction makes sociopath a more appropriate diagnosis for our society. By disengaging the conscience, unconditional self-acceptance is promoting sociopathic tendencies in both individuals and our nation as a whole. Through its emphasis on unconditional acceptance, our entire culture functions as a permissive parent that breeds unconditional self-acceptance, which leads to the deactivation of the conscience. This in turn is generating sociopathic personality tendencies within individuals and in society as a whole.

I am not suggesting that every American is a certifiable sociopath. I am asserting, however, that as parents seek to accept their children unconditionally, as teachers do likewise with their students, as therapists encourage clients toward unconditional acceptance, as many government policies reflect unconditional acceptance, as the news and entertainment industries convey the right of the individual to be accepted unconditionally, people are internalizing this message and accepting themselves unconditionally, which in turn is blunting the conscience of the individual and society, making it easier for people to function without guilt.

Those privileged with a strong Christian background or who by nature are more morally sensitive stand a better chance of maintaining an intact conscience. On the other hand, individuals with a natural inclination toward breaking rules and who also lack discipline in their homes and classrooms are at risk of expressing sociopathic behaviors. Although every society includes people with sociopathic tendencies, the promotion of unconditional self-acceptance has increased the prevalence and intensity of this inclination in our society to dangerous levels.

This blunting of our societal conscience manifests itself in many societal trends such as the prevalence of extramarital affairs that devastate spouses and children. The more virulent strains of sociopathology show themselves in school shootings, workplace violence, and mass murders that have proliferated in contemporary America. To unleash selfishness is bad enough, but to extinguish the conscience, removing the restraints of guilt and natural human empathy, produces behaviors that are cruel, heartless, and terrifying.

The Larger Experiment

America has adopted unconditional acceptance as its foundational moral principle and way of life, unleashing selfishness on our society. What results has this produced?

Society in Crisis

One day while scanning stations on my car radio, I stumbled across a talk show hosted by a therapist just as Nancy shared her story. "I am divorced and live with my children and my boyfriend Bill. I just learned that Bill molested the children of his previous wife. Now I worry for the safety of my children. To make matters worse, I am pregnant." As I listened, I felt tears welling up in my eyes, not only for Nancy and her children, but for countless callers with equally troubling stories, and for our nation as a whole, which we might view as a composite caller devastated by the emotional, behavioral, and relational chaos produced by our subjectivist, Rogerian culture. The selfishness it engenders is producing untold personal, relational, and societal chaos and pain. Agape has become a scarce commodity.

Around the 1990s Americans woke up to the depth and permanence of our post-Christian culture. The philosophical orientation of the hippie movement perpetuated by Rogers' promotion of unconditional acceptance had taken root. The Reagan era was over and Bill Clinton, a poster child for our new culture, occupied the White House.

This realization prompted a rash of books warning about the negative impact of America's new cultural orientation. The list below includes just a few of them:

- Allan Bloom: *The Closing of the American Mind* (1987) •
  David Barton: *America: To Pray or Not to Pray?* (1988) •
  James Davison Hunter:
    o *Culture Wars: The Struggle to Define America*
      (1991) o *The Death of Character: Moral Education
      in an Age without Good or Evil* (2000)
- William J. Bennett:
    o *The De-Valuing of America: The Fight for Our
      Culture and Our Children* (1992) o *The Index of
      Leading Cultural Indicators: Facts and Figures on the
      State of American Society* (1994)

- ○ *The Death of Outrage: Bill Clinton and the Assault on American Ideals* (1998)
- Myron Magnet: *The Dream and the Nightmare: the 60s Legacy to the Underclass* (1993)
- Gertrude Himmelfarb: *The De-Moralization of Society: From Victorian Virtues to Modern Values* (1994)
- Robert H. Bork: *Slouching Towards Gomorrah: Modern Liberalism and American Decline* (1996)
- Barbara Defoe Whitehead: *The Divorce Culture* (1996)

These and many other resources portray our societal decline. Much of it relates to morality. However, this erosion affects every aspect of our national life including but not limited to emotional and physical well-being, government, the economy, education, and the family.

Bert M. Farias summarizes the drastic decline in major aspects of American life across half a century as follows:

> The divorce rate has doubled, teen suicide has tripled, reported violent crime has quadrupled, the prison population has quintupled, the percentage of babies born out of wedlock has risen sixfold, couples living together out of wedlock have increased sevenfold....

> There has never been a society in the history of mankind whose moral values have deteriorated so dramatically, in such a short period of time, as those of Americans in the last 50 years.[73]

This description reveals the prevalence of selfishness and the scarcity of agape in contemporary American society. Virtually every one of these traits can be traced to those causes. These numbers do not include the catastrophic decline of our economy, our educational system, and other dimensions of our society. Most arresting is Farias' concluding claim that our society has fallen farther, faster than any society in all human history.

Linking Societal Decline with Subjectivism and Rogerianism

This book makes the case that subjectivism and

Rogerianism have produced this outcome. Several factors make this connection.

Distinct parallels between the outcome of Rogers' experiment and these developments in our society suggest that our cultural commitment to unconditional acceptance drives this decline. The timing also links these negative trends to Rogers' theory. This decay began at the time subjectivism, Rogerian psychology, and the resulting commitment to unconditional acceptance began to assume a dominant role in our society.

A rational relationship also exists between this societal decay and unconditional acceptance. Earlier in the book, we saw that the successful culture is one that promotes agape production. A society that has adopted unconditional acceptance as its sole moral principle and way of life gives license to selfishness and therefore undermines agape production. This constitutes a formula for widespread and precipitous societal disintegration.

If we unconditionally accept promiscuous sexual behavior, we should anticipate a rise in illegitimacy and divorce. If we unconditionally accept bad behavior and poor work in the classroom, we should expect declining educational outcomes. Accepting cohabitation would lead to its increase. Since these results occurred when unconditional acceptance gained prominence, it is reasonable to attribute them to its influence.

We have also seen that relationships require conditions for health and survival. Therefore, unconditional acceptance, the eradication of conditions, must bear responsibility for relational decline. Likewise, the promotion of unconditional self-acceptance links directly to the epidemic increase of sociopathic behaviors in American society.

Consequently, we have good reason to assign these catastrophic societal trends to the replacement of our agape-producing Christian culture with a selfishness-promoting one molded by subjectivism and Rogerianism. Ideas have consequences.

America Today

Between Two Cultures

This culture shift exercised a more dominant impact in certain geographical areas, influencing the Northeast and the West Coast more than the heartland. University students received an especially strong dose of indoctrination. Those with a liberal bent soak it up like a sponge, while those with a conservative orientation have displayed some resistance.

Nor has the advance of subjectivism and Rogerianism been chronologically uniform. The Reagan years returned America to a semblance of our previous Christian culture with its emphasis on responsibility and decency, a legacy that lingered briefly during the presidency of George H. W. Bush.

A major segment of American society still finds itself drawn to that traditional America with its morality, responsibility, stability, decency, and strength. That segment is also attracted by the order and success engendered by traditional American culture. This group includes a majority of evangelicals but many others also. Their rejection of contemporary culture demonstrated itself in the election of President Trump. They are desperately hoping that he will be able to reinstate elements of traditional American culture at least to some extent.

However, the left controls the news and entertainment media, our educational system, much of the judiciary, and the deep state. The result is an America divided, with the left continuing to advance its agenda, while conservatives desperately seek to prevent continued encroachment on our culture.

The Trump Effect

Americans desiring to see the subjectivist agenda stopped and a return to a moral, common-sense culture have found themselves without representation. The emergence of Donald Trump, however, has given them hope that he will represent their cause.

Trump inspires this confidence because in large measure he was not shaped by subjectivism. His mother came from a strong Christian background. His father, a hard-nosed businessman, had a major influence on his life. In *The Art of the Deal* Trump reflects, "I learned a lot from him. I learned about toughness in a very tough business, I learned about motivating people, and I learned about competence and efficiency: get in, get it done, get it done right, and get out."[74] Beginning with eighth-grade, Trump's father sent him to New York Military Academy. Regarding that experience, Trump recalls, "I stayed through my senior year, and along the way I learned a lot about discipline, and about channeling my aggression into achievement. In my senior year I was appointed a captain of the cadets."[75]

Therefore, Trump grew up in a very non-subjectivist environment that confronted him with reality and required disciplines of mind and will rather than encouraging capitulation to feelings. The demands of business have also mandated that he stay grounded in reality. None of these influences taught him that he had a right to do his own thing, that he should do what feels good, or that he would be accepted unconditionally.

Pres. Trump brings this no-nonsense orientation to government, as opposed to the subjectivism and Rogerianism that shapes the political class. Though his supporters may not identify the basis for their confidence as I have just defined it, they nonetheless sense that Pres. Trump's approach is rooted in traditional American values of rationality, responsibility, and morality in contrast with the feel-good subjectivist agenda of the left. They view his rational approach to life and government as a rock of stability in the midst of the surrounding culture of feel-good quicksand.

His approach to governance displays agape in many ways. He has shown a commitment to keep his word, which represents a major manifestation of agape. He also promotes responsibility, another trait of agape. His commitment to our military and police, and consequently our safety, embodies a form of agape. Likewise, his opposition to abortion represents a vast expression of agape towards not only unborn babies but also our society as a whole.

Pres. Trump offers more traditional, rationally rooted Americans hope through applying non-subjectivist reason and discipline in policies on immigration, reduction of burdensome regulations, reduced taxes, rebuilding our military, quelling global unrest, and confronting other problems facing our nation. In addition, he conveys disregard for the irrational subjectivist concepts promoted through political correctness.

The Missing Ingredient

However, political solutions by themselves cannot effectively combat the progressive assault on our nation. Lasting societal change demands the reinstatement of our Christian, agape-producing culture. Since only the evangelical church can achieve that objective, it constitutes America's last best hope.

The chapters ahead, however, show how the infiltration of secular culture that gives license to selfishness has left evangelicals too weak to engage effectively in the culture war. Because evangelical Christianity does represent our last best hope, the most pressing issue of our day is to expose this infiltration by secular culture and to provide a road to restoration of agape-producing, biblical Christianity within the evangelical church. Those objectives comprise the topics of the chapters ahead.

SECTION FOUR
EVANGELICAL INFILTRATION
AND THE IMPACT

The previous two sections described the secular ideology of subjectivism and its psychological form embodied in the theory of Carl Rogers. The previous section also showed the connection between subjectivism and the unconditional love and acceptance advocated by Carl Rogers. This section shows how the concept of unconditional love and acceptance has infiltrated evangelical culture, describes the form it takes, and provides a biblical analysis.

Some aspects of culture are neutral and harmless. Others are corrupt and harmful. For example, cultural architectural trends have little consequence for spiritual and moral issues or production of agape. On the other hand, sexual trends can profoundly influence the well-being of a society and its capacity to produce agape. Therefore, it is essential to determine which cultural elements to embrace and which to reject.

Doing so becomes especially challenging since, as noted earlier, for most people culture becomes truth. Therefore, they tend to view even its negative elements as good. For example, secular society has adopted cohabitation as a valid arrangement, despite its harmful effects.

As Francis Schaeffer noted, even evangelicals, though committed to the authority of Scripture, manifest the inclination to squeeze Scripture into the mold of harmful secular cultural trends. This section demonstrates how contemporary evangelicals have reshaped biblical Christianity to accommodate unconditional love and acceptance. It also demonstrates the unbiblical nature of this concept, and specifically how it accommodates and encourages selfishness.

Chapter 1: Evangelical Infiltration and Its New Belief System

This book contends that the weakness of the evangelical church and its inability to engage in the culture war result from the infiltration of our secular cultural ideology, which licenses selfishness. This assertion raises the questions of how this ideology infiltrated the evangelical belief system and what form it has taken within the evangelical context. This chapter addresses those issues.

Avenues of Infiltration

Beginning with the 1960s, subjectivist and Rogerian concepts began to infiltrate the evangelical worldview. They entered through three primary channels.

Jesus People

Hippies who responded to the gospel spawned the Jesus People movement. Though splintered and diverse, this movement manifested some common themes. It maintained many external hippie features such as dress. Many Jesus People also continued hippie behaviors. Jim Doop, a Jesus People leader, reflected years later: "They never considered that there was anything wrong with smoking [pot]."[76] The Jesus People retained the hippie mode of music, adapting it for their worship and elevating it to its own genre, which became a major element of the music industry. A July 1971 *Time* magazine cover story reported that: "'Music, the lingua franca of the young,' was the 'special medium of the Jesus movement.'"[77] In addition to these external tendencies, the Jesus People also continued to embrace many of the attitudes and concepts of hippie ideology.

Different groups of Jesus People had varying degrees of relationships with traditional churches. Chuck Smith of Calvary Chapel in Costa Mesa tailored his church program to accommodate them. Initially many Jesus People groups had little connection with traditional Christianity. However, undesirable cult-like traits that developed within the Children of God, a major Jesus People group, made those in the Jesus People movement realize their need for the stability provided by a relationship with the traditional church.[78] In addition, the demise of the hippie movement after only five years left the Jesus People culturally stranded, prompting their gravitation toward the traditional church.

Jesus People also developed ties to the evangelical church through their appeal to non-hippie evangelical young people. Jesus People attracted these church kids with their music and overt Christian commitment, and also because these church kids viewed them as cool. For them, Jesus People provided the best of both worlds: Christian commitment packaged in relevant culture.

Because Jesus People maintained attitudes and practices of the hippie culture, they imported these influences as they connected with the traditional church.

Evangelical Infiltration and Its New Belief System

Baby Boomer Influence

The Baby boomer generation absorbed the ideas, attitudes, and values of subjectivism and Rogerianism through educational institutions, music, movies, television, and culture in general. As a result, both Baby Boomers already identified with the church and also those entering from secular society brought with them the influence of secular ideology. That cultural influence produced evangelical trends such as contemporary Christian music, more relaxed dress, aversion to structure and authority, and greater emphasis on feelings. As Baby Boomers moved into positions of church leadership, these influences became dominant. For example, their resistance to structure led to the downplay of a focus on membership in many contemporary evangelical churches.

Many have observed the disproportionate influence of Baby Boomers over American society. They also exercised a disproportionate impact within the evangelical church, resulting in the acceptance of the subjectivist and Rogerian inclinations they brought with them from secular culture.

The Emergence of Evangelical Psychology

Beginning with the 1960s evangelical psychology became a dominant force within the evangelical community. Initially, evangelicals displayed resistance to psychology because of secular concepts embedded in it. The advent of a number of Christian psychologists possessing both psychological credentials and evangelical beliefs alleviated those fears. Evangelicals assumed that these psychologists would filter out unbiblical perspectives.

Evangelical psychology received an enthusiastic welcome because pastors and other evangelical leaders prior to the 1960s gave little attention to practical issues such as emotional and relational problems. Evangelical psychologists provided professional help in those areas. This arrangement resulted in evangelical psychologists exercising substantial influence.

At the time when evangelical psychology was gaining prominence, the theory of Carl Rogers was dominating secular psychology. This resulted in Rogers' theory comprising a major emphasis of the training received by most Christian psychologists, even those trained in Christian institutions. Therefore, evangelical psychologists were strongly influenced by Rogers' thinking.

Many of these evangelical psychologists believed they detected compatibility between Rogers' concepts and a biblical worldview, a correlation we will describe shortly. This connection provided a wide avenue for the infiltration of Rogers' concepts into evangelical thinking.

The Contemporary Evangelical Belief System

Jesus People, Baby boomers, and evangelical psychologists infused the evangelical worldview with a subjectivist, Rogerian orientation. Identifying those concepts effectively requires citing authors who advocate them. Without such quotes, the reader may legitimately question the validity of my concerns. Many of the sources I cite are highly visible evangelicals. I do not quote these specific people because their pronouncements are especially egregious. To the contrary, I quote them because their views reflect common themes within the contemporary evangelical community.

I want to emphasize that I hold those whom I quote in high regard. They have had extensive ministries for the Lord that have blessed countless people. Though they may have adopted unbiblical cultural concepts in one area, in practically every case these individuals hold biblical positions in other areas. God has used them to achieve great things and touch many lives. Some of them have had a significant ministry in my own life. I urge the reader to view the quotes that follow from that perspective.

That said, however, I believe that the views identified by the citations below represent erroneous perspectives that are weakening the evangelical church by eroding its production of agape. This is resulting in its failure to effectively engage in the culture war. Even great ministries can have blind spots. Consequently, these issues need to be addressed

God Loves and Accepts Human Beings Unconditionally

We observed that unconditional acceptance comprises the core of Carl Rogers' theory. It has also become a dominant theme in therapy, education, government policies, and other elements of our society. Of greatest importance, as noted earlier, it has become our secular society's sole moral principle and a way of life.

Through the channels described above, unconditional acceptance found its way into contemporary evangelical culture. It has become a dominant factor in the contemporary evangelical belief system. It shapes the contemporary evangelical understanding of their relationship with God and other human beings. It shapes their perspectives on the gospel and Christian living. Reflecting Rogers' perspective, contemporary evangelicals view unconditional acceptance and unconditional love as synonymous and interchangeable. Though evangelicals employ both terms, they use unconditional love more frequently.

Practically all prominent contemporary evangelicals assert that God loves and accepts people unconditionally and that consequently we should also love and accept ourselves and others unconditionally. Steven Furtick, in his book
(Un)Qualified: How God Uses Broken People to Do Big Things, provides an overview of the book in the first chapter. In it, he asserts that the first step in viewing ourselves as qualified is grasping "God's unconditional acceptance of you."[79] This foundational theme of God's unconditional acceptance is accentuated throughout the book. His second step entails "your acceptance of yourself, including your weaknesses,"[80] which in essence comprises unconditional self-acceptance. Furtick's teachings reflect the perspectives of the overwhelming majority of contemporary evangelicals.

David Jeremiah's book, *God Loves You: He Always Has—He Always Will*, embodies the theme of God's unconditional love and acceptance in the title. If God always has and always will love us, this assertion necessarily eliminates any conditions for that love. Therefore, this title, without using the term, asserts God's unconditional love.

Jeremiah further expresses this unconditional love and acceptance by God, again without using the term, as follows:

> I have studied the love that God has for his children, following the rich pageant of His pursuit from the Old to New Testaments, and time after time I was moved to tears by the majesty, the grace, the staggering insistence of
> His abiding affection for every citizen on Planet Earth.[81]

Scripture and history record many acts of rebellion and wickedness by human beings against God and other people, yet Jeremiah's statement contends that these in no way influenced God's love for and acceptance of them. Despite these behaviors, God maintains "staggering insistence" on loving "every citizen on Planet Earth." Therefore, God's love and acceptance of every human being must be unconditional.

He conveys the same message in these terms:

> I have a burden to tell you that God is love, and that He deeply, stubbornly, and eternally insists on loving every individual on the face of the planet. It doesn't matter who you are or what you have done. As speaker and author Max Lucado has said, "You can't fall beyond His love.".... And He doesn't merely like you when you do well. He is personally and passionately committed to your good, even when you fail.[82]

Identifying every human being as an object of God's love and asserting that His love extends throughout all of time represents yet another expression of God's unconditional love.

Jeremiah conveys similar sentiments as follows:

> His love remains intact and perfect. If you could somehow chart the love of God, it would show as a straight line across the top of the graph, never dipping, never plunging, but remaining constant, with a value of infinity. Any variance is simply imaginary, the result of our ignorance or inability to feel His love.

These assertions indicate that God's unconditional love is both of the philia type, "His abiding affection," and the agape type, "He is personally and passionately committed to your good."

Literally hundreds of other evangelical books accentuate the theme of God's unconditional love and acceptance. This concept shows itself in vast numbers of sermons, in Christian radio and television programming, in podcasts, and even in Christian music.

The prevalence of the theme of unconditional love and acceptance in both the writings of Steven Furtick, who just entered his 40s, and those of David Jeremiah, who is on the cusp of leaving his 70s, reveals the enduring nature of this concept, influencing evangelicals from the inception of the Baby Boomer generation to the present. It has become the cornerstone of contemporary evangelical culture.

We see the dominance of this theme in the absence of significant opposition. One is hard-pressed to find any prominent evangelical who challenges the biblical validity of this theme. Though some may exist, their concerns have not gained traction. Instead, evangelicals almost universally believe that God's unconditional love and acceptance comprises biblical truth. Questioning its veracity is viewed as heresy.

The Broad Implications of Unconditional Love and Acceptance

Our discussion of Carl Rogers revealed that unconditional acceptance possesses vast implications for morality, relationships, and other aspects of life. It wields no less significance in the evangelical context but rather is amplified because evangelicals teach that God extends unconditional love and acceptance. This belief vastly magnifies its consequences. Contemporary evangelicals assert that because God accepts us unconditionally, we should accept one another unconditionally, extending this concept to the horizontal plane.

Contemporary evangelicals, reflecting the teaching of Rogers, view failure to grasp God's unconditional acceptance as a major cause of emotional, behavioral, and relational problems. Assuring hurting people of God's unconditional love and acceptance brings healing and resolves problems. Consequently, the concept of unconditional love and acceptance exercises vast influence on evangelical thinking and living.

The Source of the Concept of Unconditional Love and Acceptance

The terms unconditional love or unconditional acceptance are not found in Scripture but, as we have seen, represent the foundational concept of secular culture. The chapter ahead analyzes whether these concepts are scriptural. However, there can be little doubt that evangelicals did not derive them from Scripture but borrowed them from secular culture, and that they made their way into the evangelical belief system through the channels described above.

One reason to identify secular culture as the source of evangelical belief in unconditional acceptance resides in the timing of its evangelical appearance. It surfaced shortly after its embrace as a major secular theme. If it were a scriptural concept, Christians would have adopted it centuries ago. They did not. Likewise, its adoption at the time when evangelical psychologists, trained in Rogerian theory, gained prominence also suggests its secular roots.

The Linchpin

Contemporary evangelicals view unconditional love and acceptance as biblical because they view it as expressing the biblical concept of grace. God's grace entails His acceptance of us apart from works, which seems to convey unconditional acceptance. Philip Yancey in his book *What's So Amazing About Grace?* addresses this theme of grace by asserting, "Only Christianity dares to make God's love unconditional,"[83] thus linking grace and unconditional love. He includes a quote from counselor David Seamands that expresses the relationship between grace and unconditional love from the negative perspective as follows.

> Many years ago I was driven to the conclusion that the two major causes of most emotional problems among evangelical Christians are these: the failure to understand, receive, and live out God's unconditional grace and forgiveness; and the failure to give out that unconditional love, forgiveness, and grace to other people.[84]

This equating of grace with unconditional love and acceptance is often not expressed explicitly but instead conveyed using other terms. For example, Yancey says,

> Grace makes its appearance in so many forms that I have trouble defining it. I am ready, though, to attempt something like a definition of grace in relation to God. Grace means there is nothing we can do to make God love us more—no amount of spiritual calisthenics and renunciations, no amount of knowledge gained from seminaries and divinity schools, no amount of crusading on behalf of righteous causes. And grace means there is nothing we can do to make God love us less—no amount of racism or pride or pornography or adultery or even murder. Grace means that God already loves us as much as an infinite God can possibly love."[85]

By asserting that because of grace, no human behavior could possibly alter God's love for us, Yancey equates God's grace with unconditional love and acceptance.

This represents a widely and fervently held position of the contemporary evangelical community. In fact, almost any extended contemporary evangelical discussion on grace will almost invariably incorporate the term unconditional acceptance or unconditional love. Consequently, the evangelical and Rogerian systems, though rooted in diametrically distinct worldviews, one theocentric and the other humanistic, appear to converge in the core concept of each, the evangelical belief in grace and the Rogerian commitment to unconditional acceptance. Since grace comprises the core concept of the evangelical worldview and unconditional acceptance forms the centerpiece of Rogers' theory, equating these two concepts links secular and evangelical culture.

Equating grace with unconditional love and acceptance does not merely provide us with a more contemporary name for grace. Rather, it loads grace with the vast implications of unconditional acceptance that we identified in our study of Rogers. Because grace comprises a foundational evangelical concept, expanding its meaning significantly influences the entire evangelical belief system.

Performance Not Required

God's unconditional acceptance means that nothing I do will negatively influence God's attitude or actions toward me. This perspective has led to the contemporary evangelical position that the believer does not need to "perform" to please God. Since God accepts him unconditionally, how he lives, his "performance," will not alter God's acceptance. Regarding the Christian life, Philip Yancey reflects: "By instinct I feel I must *do something* in order to be accepted."[86] He then states his perspective on Christian living as follows: "The world runs by ungrace. Everything depends on what I do....Jesus' kingdom calls us to another way, one that depends not on our performance but his own."[87]

Yancey views grace, unconditional acceptance, as freeing the believer from the obligation to perform. Pleasing God is not dependent on anything he does, but only on what Christ has done for him.

Tim Keller expresses the contemporary evangelical position this way:

> God imputes Christ's perfect performance to us as if it were our own, and adopts us into His family. In other words, God can say to us just as He once said to Christ, 'You are my Son, whom I love; with you I am well pleased.'
>
> You see, the verdict is in. And now I perform on the basis of the verdict. Because He loves me and He accepts me, I do not have to do things just to build up my résumé. I do not have to do things to make me look good. I can do things for the joy of doing them. I can help people to help people – not so I can feel better about myself, not so I can fill up the emptiness.[88]

Keller is asserting that God's verdict regardless of our lifestyle is, "You are my Son, whom I love; with you I am well pleased." Consequently, we do not practice biblical behaviors to please God and receive His blessing, but we now "perform," do loving deeds, just "for the joy of doing them."

This assertion that the believer does not need to perform to enjoy God's favor has become a major theme of the contemporary evangelical church. Attend almost any contemporary evangelical church or event, and before long this cliché will surface. And when it does, it is invariably greeted by an animated audience response, revealing that this concept powerfully resonates with them.

Contemporary evangelicals support this teaching with the companion assertion that when God looks on us he does not see our behavior but the righteousness of Christ. Consequently, they contend that our behavior, our performance, in no way influences God's attitude or actions toward us.

The assurance that we do not need to perform to please God has far-reaching implications. It connotes that the believer's lifestyle, whatever that includes, will in no way diminish his fellowship with God, lead to God's chastening, result in unanswered prayers, negatively affect God's use of him in ministry, or inhibit God's blessing and reward.

The Enemy

Legalism comprises the antagonist of the contemporary evangelical church. Since God accepts us unconditionally, which eliminates the need to "perform" to enjoy His acceptance, contemporary evangelicals view any conditions needed to please the Lord as legalism. In addition, they view conditions as comprising a basis for judgmentalism, since conditions provide a standard with which to judge others whereas unconditional acceptance eliminates any premise for judging.

Reflecting the theory of Carl Rogers, contemporary evangelicals assert that experiencing unconditional acceptance from God and others produces health, peace, and growth while the legalistic demand for performance brings failure and guilt. Manifesting grace, unconditional acceptance, is Christ-like; legalism is Pharisee-like. Therefore, maintaining a healthy church environment requires vigilance to identify and remove any expression of legalism and the judgmentalism it produces.

Chuck Swindoll passionately expresses this view of legalism as the enemy. After reflecting on the desire for freedom possessed by all human beings, Swindoll asserts:

> And it is every bit as true for God's people who have existed too long in the suffocating grip of legalistic demands and expectations. Long enough have those who wish to control and intimidate others in the body of Christ been allowed to do so. I am pleased to announce that their grip is loosening as grace is awakening.[89]

This quote not only identifies legalism as the enemy but also shows it to be a hallmark of the traditional evangelical perspective from which contemporary evangelicals are breaking free. This perspective is widely held among evangelicals. Often one hears an evangelical speaker refer to his legalistic childhood. They conclude that these traditional evangelicals practiced legalism because they failed to understand the true nature of grace, that it entails unconditional acceptance.

It seems that a secular psychologist, Carl Rogers, opened evangelical eyes to a valid understanding of grace as consisting of unconditional acceptance, which eliminates the need to "perform." Or as an evangelical counselor friend shared with me, "It seems that Rogers stumbled across a foundational biblical truth," one we were too blinded by our own legalism to see.

It is important to understand that now legalism does not merely encompass traditional evangelical taboos against behaviors such as drinking alcoholic beverages, attendance at movies, and dancing. Rather, under the influence of unconditional acceptance, legalism includes citing any restriction or requirement as a condition for pleasing God, even ones identified in Scripture. Unconditional acceptance and the companion belief that we do not need to perform to please God requires this position on legalism.

Agape production

Of course, contemporary evangelicals care about how believers live and want them to manifest agape toward God and our neighbor. They believe, however, that agape results not from keeping rules but by the experience of God's unconditional love and acceptance. Contemporary evangelicals teach that the experience of this unconditional, nonperformance acceptance will result in the believer spontaneously displaying agape, not because he "ought to," because the rules say he must, but because he "wants to." Notice the parallel of this position to the theory of Carl Rogers. Both assert that the experience of unconditional acceptance will spontaneously produce appropriate behavior.

A Diagram Summarizing the Contemporary Evangelical Position

Earlier I diagrammed the theory of Carl Rogers as follows:

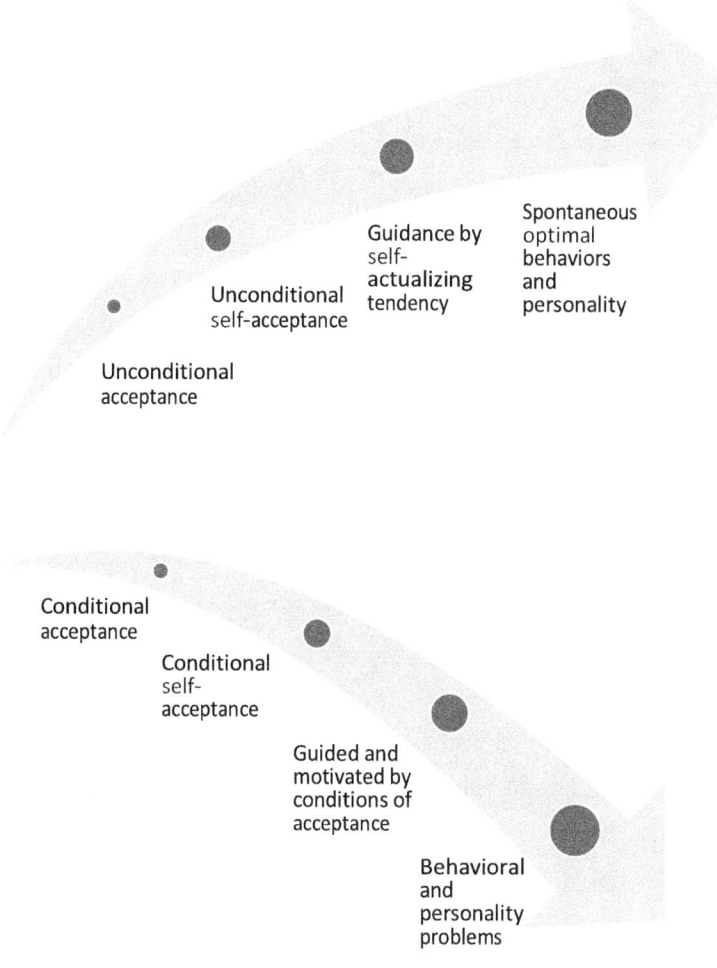

Unconditional
acceptance

Unconditional
self-acceptance

Guidance by
self-
actualizing
tendency

Spontaneous
optimal
behaviors
and
personality

Conditional
acceptance

Conditional
self-
acceptance

Guided and
motivated by
conditions of
acceptance

Behavioral
and
personality
problems

We might diagram the contemporary evangelical position as follows:

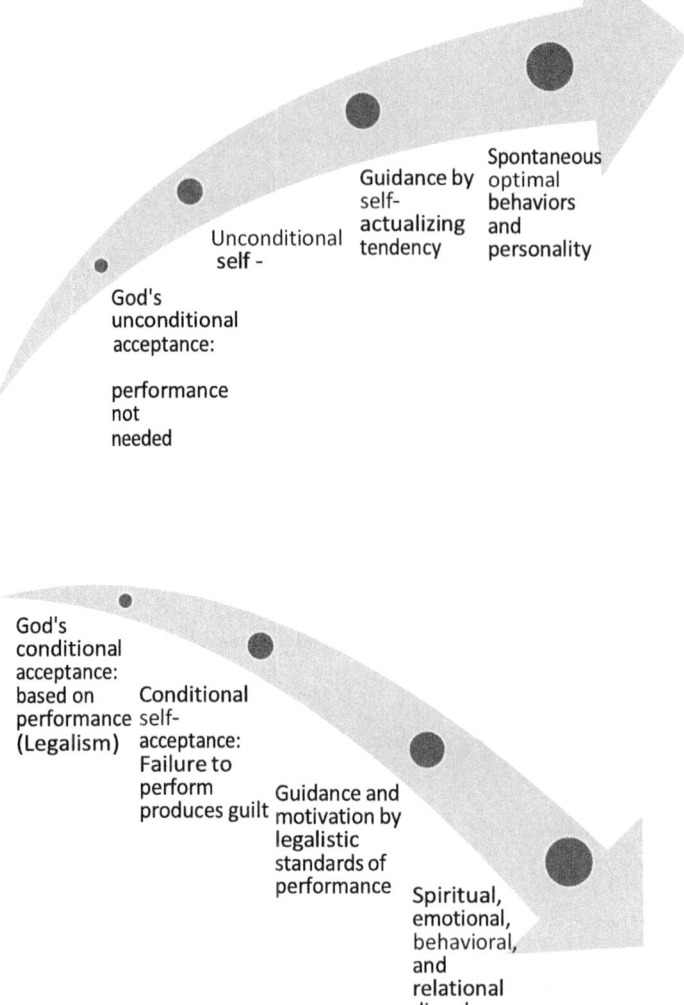

God's
unconditional
acceptance:

performance
not
needed

Unconditional
self -

Guidance by
self-
actualizing
tendency

Spontaneous
optimal
behaviors
and
personality

God's
conditional
acceptance:
based on
performance
(Legalism)

Conditional
self-
acceptance:
Failure to
perform
produces guilt

Guidance and
motivation by
legalistic
standards of
performance

Spiritual,
emotional,
behavioral,
and
relational
disorders

Notice the parallels between these two positions. The striking resemblance further demonstrates that the contemporary evangelical belief system finds its source in the theory of Carl Rogers.

Distinctions between Traditional and Contemporary Evangelical Belief Systems

The contemporary evangelical beliefs just described result in a new evangelical view of the Christian life that differs significantly from the traditional evangelical perspective that dominated evangelical thinking up until several decades ago. Traditional and contemporary evangelicals hold many of the same core beliefs. However, the views just described drastically change the evangelical perspective on our relationship with God and how He intends the Christian life to work. The following describes those profound differences.

The Traditional Evangelical Perspective on Christian Living

Historically evangelicals held that God's commandments to love Him and one another required that the believer maintain a godly lifestyle and serve Him faithfully. Doing so pleased Him and resulted in His blessing and reward. Failing to do so led to His chastening.

Contrary to contemporary assessments of traditional evangelicals, they did not view God as harsh and unloving, ready and eager to pounce on any believer who got out of line. Perhaps some did, but that perspective did not describe the dominant traditional attitude. Rather they saw Him as a loving God who chastened believers in order to maintain His own holiness and the purity of His church, and also to prevent them from perpetuating destructive behaviors. They viewed God as gracious and forgiving toward those who confess their sins. However, they believed God's chastening could be severe toward those who continue down a sinful path.

Some traditional groups added rules beyond those found in Scripture. In most cases, these comprised attempts to apply biblical principles to contemporary cultural problems. For example, they viewed movies as a Trojan horse that promoted godless concepts and behaviors. That concern seems to have been well-founded. Nonetheless, for a church to legislate in these areas might be viewed as unbiblical in that it robs believers of freedom to make their own assessment.

In summary, they believed that God deals with us based on our performance, blessing and rewarding those who maintain biblical behaviors and chastening those who do not. Therefore, they viewed exhorting believers to maintain godly behaviors as a biblical responsibility and not legalism.

The Contemporary Evangelical Perspective on Christian Living

Contemporary evangelicals embrace a diametrically opposite set of perspectives on these issues. They assert that God loves us unconditionally. When He looks on us, He does not see our sins but the righteousness of Christ. Since we already have His full acceptance, we do not need to perform to please Him. Rather, our motivation to display agape toward Him and others stems from the realization that we are already unconditionally accepted.

They view seeking to maintain even biblical rules in order to gain God's acceptance as legalistic. They contend that this legalistic approach cannot and will not produce a genuine Christian life characterized by freedom, joy, and agape. Instead will produce joyless, pharisaical Christians who represent a deformed expression of Christian living that drives people away from the gospel and the church.

They believe it is important for Christians to behave biblically but contend that we will do so in response to our experience of God's unconditional acceptance. They further maintain that we should not be motivated to fix areas of failure by concern regarding God's disapproval, since this only brings us back under the legalistic, performance-based traditional evangelical perspective. Rather, as the individual continues to bask in the sunshine of God's grace, His unconditional love and acceptance, and receives corresponding unconditional love and acceptance by other believers, he will ultimately develop the desire to spontaneously live biblically in those areas.

We find these perspectives propagated by practically every segment of the contemporary evangelical community. They are especially prominent in mega-churches. In fact, they might legitimately be viewed as the hallmark of contemporary evangelical Christianity.

How important are these differences?

If the traditional perspective is wrong, if it produces warped, pharisaical believers bound by legalism, robbed of joy, and failing to produce agape, it is good that evangelicals have rejected it. And if the contemporary perspective offers freedom and a biblical approach to transformation that spontaneously produces agape, then it is essential to embrace it.

If, however, the traditional perspective is biblical, then performing to maintain God's favor represents a biblical motivation that contributes significantly to Christian living. Consequently, teaching that God accepts us unconditionally, apart from performance, undercuts an essential biblical motivation to generate agape, instead freeing our sinful nature to produce selfish behaviors.

Therefore, it is imperative that we determine which of these perspectives is rooted in Scripture. Since they are diametrically opposite, they cannot both be biblical. Determining which of these positions reflects the teaching of Scripture comprises the most salient issue confronting the church today. The chapters ahead provide a biblical and rational analysis.

Chapter 2: Does God Love and Accept Unconditionally?

This chapter addresses two issues. First, it explores whether God loves and accepts all human beings unconditionally. Then it considers whether God loves and accepts believers unconditionally.

Does God Love and Accept Human Beings Unconditionally?

As noted earlier, evangelicals tend to view the terms love and accept as synonymous. However, to fully examine this issue, I treat these terms separately, first addressing the issue of God's unconditional acceptance of all human beings.

Does God Accept Human Beings Unconditionally?

The belief that God accepts people unconditionally necessarily must mean that He showers His unmitigated blessing of human beings since unconditional acceptance eliminates any basis for withholding blessing or assigning judgment.

Even a cursory reading of Scripture, however, reveals that God judges human beings often and severely, thus demonstrating that God maintains some condition for acceptance and that those being judged have not met it. Consider this sampling:

- In response to human wickedness, God brought a flood over all the earth that killed all but eight people.

- Because of their wickedness, God annihilated Sodom and Gomorrah with fire and brimstone. Only Lot and his family escaped.

- Because of the disobedience of Israel and Judah, God sent the Assyrians and Babylonians to inflict terrible devastation on them.

- Matthew 24:21 describes God's future judgment on the earth. "For then there will be great tribulation, such as has not been since the beginning of the world until this time, no, nor ever shall be" (NKJV).

- The Bible teaches that unbelievers will ultimately suffer in an eternal Hell.

Drowning almost the entire population of the earth or consuming two cities with fire and brimstone graphically conveys non-acceptance. The last two items on this list are future, demonstrating that even after the cross God continues to accept human beings conditionally.

Some may contend that though God's actions may not convey unconditional acceptance His underlying attitude does. Many passages of Scripture, however, reveal that God's attitude as well as His actions are hostile toward sinners. Hebrews 3:10 reports God's hostile attitude toward the rebellious generations of Jews coming out of Egypt. "Therefore I was provoked with that generation, and said, 'They always go astray in their heart; they have not known my ways.'" (ESV) Thayer's lexicon indicates that the Greek word for provoke can mean "to loathe" or "to be disgusted with."[90] Many other passages convey similar sentiments. Consequently, Scripture teaches that God's acceptance is conditional, regarding both His actions and His attitude.

Does God Love Human Beings Unconditionally?

Contemporary evangelicals are more prone to speak of God's unconditional love than His unconditional acceptance, love being more often used in Scripture. David Jeremiah teaches, "Most Christians are familiar with the word agape, which is a term used to describe God's unconditional love."[91] Some may contend that though God's actions described above may demonstrate God's conditional acceptance, He nonetheless loves all people unconditionally.

Psalm 5:4-6 reveals, however, that God's love is conditional.

> For you are not a God who delights in wickedness; evil may not dwell with you. The boastful shall not stand before your eyes; you hate all evildoers. You destroy those who speak lies; the LORD abhors the bloodthirsty and deceitful man. (Psalms 5:4-6)

Evangelicals tend to explain away "You hate all workers of iniquity" by asserting that "hate" means to love less. The verse that follows, however, reveals that David had the common meaning of hate in mind: "You destroy those who speak lies; the LORD abhors the bloodthirsty and deceitful man." (Psalm 5:6). God's hatred for the wicked described here includes both action and feeling types of hatred. "You shall destroy those who speak falsehood" describes God's hostile actions against the wicked. "The Lord abhors the bloodthirsty and deceitful man" describes God's negative emotions toward them. This passage makes it clear that God's wrath is antithetical to both agape, action-type love, and philia, feeling-type love.

Psalm 11:5-6 records similar sentiments:

> The LORD examines the righteous, but the wicked, those who love violence, he hates with a passion. On the wicked he will rain fiery coals and

burning sulfur; a scorching wind will be their lot.
(Psalms 11:5-6 NIV)

This passage, as with the previous one, expresses both God's hostile feelings and actions toward the wicked.

God also reflects animus toward sinners in the means of judgment He chooses. He could use lethal injection but instead employs terribly painful "fiery coals and burning sulfur" and "a scorching wind."

The assertion of these passages that God not only hates sin but also sinners shocks contemporary evangelicals. Though not in the Bible, contemporary evangelicals recite the mantra, "God hates the sin but loves the sinner" as if possessing scriptural authority. God does display love for sinners, a topic I will address shortly. Nonetheless, these passages affirm that God's love is conditional and that at times He displays hatred toward both wicked deeds and their perpetrators.

God's wrath toward the sinner is also taught in John 3:36, "He who believes in the Son has eternal life; but he who does not obey the Son will not see life, but the wrath of God abides on him" (NASB). The Greek word for "wrath" in this verse describes both an attitude of hostility and the ensuing actions. Other New Testament passages make reference to God's wrath, such as:

- Ephesians 2:3: "(A)mong whom also we all once conducted ourselves in the lusts of our flesh, fulfilling the desires of the flesh and of the mind, and were by nature children of wrath, just as the others." (NKJV)
- Ephesians 5:6: "Let no one deceive you with empty words, for because of these things the wrath of God comes upon the sons of disobedience."

In response, some cite the following New Testament passages that seem to teach God's unconditional love.

- John 3:16: "For God so loved the world, that he gave his only Son, that whoever believes in him should not perish but have eternal life."

- Romans 5:8: "(B)ut God shows his love for us in that while we were still sinners, Christ died for us."
- 1 John 4:10: "In this is love, not that we have loved God but that he loved us and sent his Son to be the propitiation for our sins."

These verses do not stipulate that God loves unconditionally. However, many conclude that they do because they indicate that God loved us even while we were in our sinful condition.

Since both the passages above speaking of God's wrath and those describing His love are included in Scripture, we must reconcile them rather than embrace one set and ignore the other. We can achieve this by identifying the specific expression of God's love that the latter group of verses has in view. They all employ the term agape, either in the noun or verb forms, therefore referring to an action by God. The verbs are in the aorist tense, which envisions an act as a whole or as a completed action as opposed to ongoing action. "He mowed the grass" versus "he is mowing the grass." Therefore, these verses refer to a specific act of love by God toward human beings. All three passages identify that act—God's sending Christ to die for our sins. Therefore, they are not teaching that God maintains an ongoing, unconditional love for human beings but rather that God performed an act of love in sending Christ to provide redemption for us. Consequently, they do not teach unconditional love.

The fact that the New Testament does not teach unconditional love is also underscored in passages such as Hebrews 10:28-31 that asserts:

> Anyone who has set aside the law of Moses dies without mercy on the evidence of two or three witnesses. How much worse punishment, do you think, will be deserved by the one who has trampled underfoot the Son of God, and has profaned the blood of the covenant by which he was sanctified, and has outraged the Spirit of

grace? For we know him who said, "Vengeance is mine; I will repay." And again, "The Lord will judge his people." It is a fearful thing to fall into the hands of the living God.

God's Love for People

The discussion above is not asserting that God has no love for human beings. Scripture tells us that God shows profound love toward us in many ways. Let me list some.

- God sends rain and sunshine even on sinful people.
- God prefers blessing to judgment. In Ezekiel 18:32 God asserts, "For I have no pleasure in the death of anyone, declares the Lord GOD; so turn, and live."
- God desires to see people saved: "The Lord is not slow to fulfill his promise as some count slowness, but is patient toward you, not wishing that any should perish, but that all should reach repentance" (2 Peter 3:9).
- God redeemed human beings at great price, giving His Son to make that possible.
- God draws people to Himself through the ministry of the Holy Spirit.

The Conditional Nature of God's Love

This far from comprehensive list clearly demonstrates God's love. The question, however, is not whether God loves people but whether He loves people unconditionally. The passages cited earlier in this chapter and many others describing God's wrath and judgment make it undeniable that God's acceptance and love are conditional. Therefore, the contemporary evangelical teaching that God loves and accepts human beings unconditionally is erroneous.

Some conclude that God loves us unconditionally based on the assertions in 1 John 4:8 and 4:16 that God is love. However, other verses assign other characteristics to God. For example, Exodus 34:14 states, "(F)or you shall worship no other god, for the LORD, whose name is Jealous, is a jealous God." Likewise,

Isaiah 6:3 does not describe the Seraphim crying, "Love, love, love is the Lord of hosts" but "Holy, holy, holy." Therefore, it is erroneous to assume that the description of God as love in two verses encompasses the entire scope of His nature, and from that to conclude that His love is unconditional.

The Takeaways

The discussion above demonstrates that the contemporary evangelical teaching that God loves and accepts all people conflicts with Scripture. This finding further suggests that evangelicals derived this concept from secular culture and not Scripture. The infiltration of unconditional love and acceptance into the evangelical worldview reflects that secular culture is exercising greater influence than Scripture in these areas. Spiritual health and vitality require that we restore the authority of Scripture in our analysis of those topics.

Does God Love and Accept Believers Unconditionally?

Our conclusion that God's love and acceptance of humanity in general is conditional leaves open the question of whether God unconditionally loves and accepts the believer. For the sake of thoroughness, the issues of God's love and His acceptance of the believer are examined separately.

Does God Love Believers Unconditionally?

David Jeremiah graphically expresses that God loves the believer unconditionally as follows:

> There is a good side and a better side to God's unchanging love. The good side is that God won't wake up in the morning and decide He's had enough of us. The better side is that even when we wake up in the morning and decide we've had enough of Him, He will still love us.[92]

The following analysis demonstrates that Scripture does not support this position.

Statements of Scripture

John 15:10 asserts: "If you keep My commandments, you will abide in My love." The related note in the Ryrie Study Bible states: "Abiding in His love is conditioned on obedience." John 14:21 embodies the same truth: "He who has My commandments and keeps them, he it is who loves Me; and he who loves Me shall be loved by My Father, and I will love him, and will disclose Myself to him" (NAS). We find a similar expression in John 14:23: "Jesus answered and said to him, 'If anyone loves Me, he will keep My word; and My Father will love him, and We will come to him, and make Our abode with him'" (NAS). The repetition of this truth confirms the conclusion that God's love for the believer is conditional.

The conditional nature of God's love for the believer is perhaps most graphically demonstrated in statements by Christ regarding His Father's conditional love for Him: "For this reason the Father loves Me, because I lay down My life that I may take it again" (John 10:17 NAS). In this verse Jesus teaches that the Father's love for Him is conditional, predicated on His doing His Father's will. Jesus conveys the same message in John 15:10: "If you keep My commandments, you will abide in My love; just as I have kept My Father's commandments, and abide in His love." Jesus clearly indicates that His abiding in His Father's love is conditioned on His keeping His Father's commandments.

Though this conclusion regarding the love of the Father for His Son may sound preposterous, these statements of Jesus are not ambiguous. Though we know that it is impossible for Jesus to sin, imagine for a second that when Satan offered Him the kingdoms of the world, to avoid the impending life of rejection culminating in the cross, Jesus had succumbed to this temptation, bowing down and worshiping Satan. In the passages just considered, Jesus is saying that doing so would have negatively altered the Father's love for Him. Or stated in the positive, the fact that Jesus never would capitulate to sin elicits a profound response of love by the Father toward Him. God loves righteousness and grace, and therefore He possesses infinite love for a Son who displayed those qualities perfectly, even when engulfed in the most horrific circumstances imaginable.

Scripture teaches that God's love for the believer is even conditioned on our attitude when giving. "So let each one give as he purposes in his heart, not grudgingly or of necessity; for God loves a cheerful giver" (2 Corinthians 9:7 NKJV). The word for love in this passage is agape, indicating that our willingness to share generously with others influences God's attitudes and actions toward us. This assertion that God loves the generous giver suggests that God's love for the believer is conditioned on our obedience to the full range of our expressions of agape toward others. This conclusion is both scriptural and countercultural. It forces us to choose whether Scripture or culture comprises our authority in determining truth.

God's Actions toward Believers

Not only do the statements of Scripture indicate that God's love for the believer is conditional, but His actions toward some believers also support this conclusion.

The conditional nature of God's love for believers manifests itself in God's taking the lives of Ananias and Sapphira in Acts 5:1-11. By today's standards, their transgression did not seem that egregious. They sold a property, contributed a part of the proceeds to the church, but told the apostles that they had donated the totality of the sale price. Nonetheless, God smote them dead for their lie.

God also took the lives of others for displaying selfishness in their observance of the Lord's supper. They were sufficiently affluent to bring a sumptuous meal for themselves but did not share with poor brothers and sisters who hungrily looked on. 1Corinthians 11:30 records, "That is why many of you are weak and ill, and some have died."

Scripture teaches that some of God's chastening is an act of love. For example, Hebrews 12:6 explains, "For the Lord disciplines the one he loves, and chastises every son whom he receives." Today we would label this as tough love. However, since agape constitutes seeking the benefit of another, God in taking the lives of Ananias and Sapphira and some of the Corinthian believers cannot be construed as tough love.

These passages demonstrate that the contemporary evangelical cliché "There is nothing you can do to make God love you more and nothing you can do to make God love you less" is not compatible with Scripture.

Passages Used to Support God's Unconditional Love for Believers

Some might argue that Romans 8:35-39 teaches that God's love for the believer is unconditional.

> Who shall separate us from the love of Christ? Shall tribulation, or distress, or persecution, or famine, or nakedness, or danger, or sword? As it is written, "For your sake we are being killed all the day long; we are regarded as sheep to be slaughtered." No, in all these things we are more than conquerors through him who loved us. For I am sure that neither death nor life, nor angels nor rulers, nor things present nor things to come, nor powers, nor height nor depth, nor anything else in all creation, will be able to separate us from the love of God in Christ Jesus our Lord.

We must reconcile this passage with all of the verses above indicating the conditional nature of God's love toward the believer. We can achieve this by noting that sin is not included in the list of those forces incapable of separating us from God's love. Paul is making the point that no force assaulting us can separate us from God's love, but he leaves open the possibility that our own sinful choices can negatively influence God's love for us. This passage is written to those who are "for your sake being killed all the day long." Therefore, Paul's purpose is not to give assurance of God's love to those living in sin but to those being persecuted.

Does God Love and Accept Unconditionally?

Some contemporary evangelicals seek to support the concept of God's unconditional love by referring to passages related to His steadfast love for Israel that ultimately prevails. While God loves Israel as a nation with an everlasting love, His love for individuals within that nation has been conditional. For example, we find God condemning and bringing terrible judgments on countless Israelites. It is not valid to draw a parallel between God's interaction with the Jewish nation as a whole and individual New Testament believers, but rather the parallel should be drawn between the nation Israel and the church, and between individual Israelites in the Old Testament and individual believers in the New Testament. This parallel supports a conditional understanding of God's love and acceptance of the individual New Testament believer.

The above discussion reveals that God shows love toward believers conditioned on their displaying agape toward Him and toward others, i.e. their keeping the First and Second Great Commandments.

Does God Accept Believers Unconditionally?

First let me assert that this discussion of acceptance is not dealing with loss of salvation but with relational issues pertaining to God's blessing, reward, fellowship, and answering our prayers. Contemporary evangelicals contend that when God views a believer, He does not see the believer's behavior but instead the righteousness of Christ. Consequently, his performance, whether loving or selfish, is not a factor in God's attitude toward us or His dealing with us.

Therefore, contemporary evangelicals conclude from their belief in God's unconditional acceptance and this teaching that we do not need to perform to please God. In other words, our lifestyle in no way influences our relationship with God or His attitude or actions toward us.

Performance can mean putting on an act. Of course, God does not want us to do that. What, then, is the nature of the performance to which Scripture calls us? He mandates that we produce agape. The First and Second Commandments and the New Commandment call us to this purpose. All the other commands merely provide specific expressions of these commands to love.

Consequently, teaching that we do not need to perform to please God in essence asserts that He is just as pleased if we produce agape or live selfishly. Using Keller's terms, the verdict is in that God continuously views the believer as His beloved child in whom He is well pleased, just as He was pleased with Christ, even if we live selfishly rather than produce agape.

The view that we do not need to perform to please God may seem like a magnanimous expression of God's grace, but it denigrates the importance and welfare of other people. It asserts that God smiles on us unconditionally even as we harm others. Our study of unconditional acceptance revealed that it assigns total importance to the person being accepted and relegates all others to the status of objects. Likewise, saying that we do not need to perform, to produce agape, to please God conveys that our unkindness toward others does not matter to God. It even connotes that our disregard for Him is irrelevant to Him. In other words, it issues a license to live selfishly.

The analysis below reveals that according to Scripture we must perform, i.e. refrain from selfishness and produce agape, in order to please God.

The Nature of Commands and Consequences for Not Obeying Them

Scriptural commands that we produce agape strongly indicates that doing so pleases God. It seems unreasonable that God is just as pleased with us regardless of whether or not we obey His commands. This teaching violates the very nature of commands. Virtually every command issued by every authority figure carries with it the implication that failing to obey it negatively influences that relationship.

Contemporary evangelicals, however, assert that when God looks on us, He does not see our negative performance but the perfect life of Christ. Consequently, He is pleased with us regardless of our performance. It is true that when we are saved our sins are forgiven and that through Christ we are justified before God as judge. However, as believers, we have an ongoing relationship with God as father in which He sees and interacts with us based on our performance.

The passages below specifically state that God's acceptance of, being pleased with, believers is determined by their production of agape.

- "For the kingdom of God is not a matter of eating and drinking but of righteousness and peace and joy in the Holy Spirit. Whoever thus serves Christ is acceptable to God and approved by men." (Romans 14:17-18)
- "Therefore we make it our aim, whether present or absent, to be well pleasing to Him." (2 Corinthians 5:9 NKJV)
- "(S)o as to walk in a manner worthy of the Lord, fully pleasing to him, bearing fruit in every good work and increasing in the knowledge of God." (Colossians 1:10)

Paul even more graphically describes God's conditional acceptance of the believer, that God's acceptance is based on performance, in 1 Corinthians 10:1-11. He does so by asserting that God's dealing with Israel in the wilderness provides an example for us.

> For I do not want you to be unaware, brothers, that our fathers were all under the cloud, and all passed through the sea, and all were baptized into Moses in the cloud and in the sea, and all ate the same spiritual food, and all drank the same spiritual drink. For they drank from the spiritual Rock that followed them, and the Rock was Christ. Nevertheless, with most of them God was not pleased, for they were overthrown in the wilderness. Now these things took place as examples for us, that we might not desire evil as they did. Do not be idolaters as some of them were; as it is written, "The people sat down to eat and drink and rose up to

> play." We must not indulge in sexual immorality as
> some of them did, and twenty-three thousand fell in
> a single day. We must not put Christ to the test, as
> some of them did and were destroyed by serpents,
> nor grumble, as some of them did and were
> destroyed by the Destroyer. Now these things
> happened to them as an example, but they were
> written down for our instruction, on whom the end
> of the ages has come.

Paul recounts that God took the lives of a large number of these Israelites, which provides a vivid display of nonacceptance. Paul explicitly identifies God's attitude of nonacceptance in stating that God was "not pleased" with those who sinned. In this passage, Paul states twice that this story serves as an example for us, indicating that God's acceptance of New Testament believers is also related to their behavior.

Note that God not only took the lives of these Israelites for behaviors we tend to view as spiritual felonies like idolatry, but also for those we might consider misdemeanors such as grumbling. Paul's observation that God was not pleased "with *most of them*" warns that God might be displeased with us even if our behaviors reflect the evangelical majority. These consequences convey that God is pleased when we obey, when we produce agape, and displays His dissatisfaction when we live selfishly.

In summary, Scripture indicates by teaching and example that we are not only obligated to perform, but also that God displays an unfavorable attitude and disciplinary actions toward us when we fail to do so. Scripture also affirms the positive side of this equation, that producing agape results in His blessing and reward, like a boss giving an employee who performs well a promotion or year-end bonus.

Some might contend that God accepts the believer but not his inappropriate behavior. We noted earlier that this perspective, distinguishing between the person and his behavior, is not scriptural. In addition, the passages above refer not only to behaviors being pleasing to the Lord but persons, e.g. "Therefore we make it our aim, whether present or absent, to be well pleasing to Him." Beyond that, God in taking the life of believers conveys in the most unambiguous terms nonacceptance of both behaviors and persons.

The New Testament Emphasizes the Need to Perform from One End to the Other

The contemporary evangelical assertion that we do not need to perform to please God is problematic because performance represents a major theme from one end of the New Testament to the other.

- John the Baptist emphasized performance as did Jesus in the Sermon on the Mount
- Romans 12-15 is filled with exhortations to perform.
- Paul devotes most of the book of 1Corinthians to rebuking the Corinthians for their poor performance and instructing them to instead produce agape, culminating in the love chapter of 1 Corinthians 13.
- Some might contend that the New Testament's emphasis on grace eliminates the need for the believer to perform. Galatians, which probably emphasizes the theme of grace more than any other New Testament book, includes passages such as the following: "Now the works of the flesh are evident: sexual immorality, impurity, sensuality, idolatry, sorcery, enmity, strife, jealousy, fits of anger, rivalries, dissensions, divisions, envy, drunkenness, orgies, and things like these. I warn you, as I warned you before, that those who do such things will not inherit the kingdom of God." (Galatians 5:19-21)
- Practically every New Testament book includes a call to performance, culminating in the letters to the seven churches in Revelation 2-3, which place substantial emphasis on performance and the dire consequences for

failure to perform. For example, Christ warned the church of Ephesus: "Remember therefore from where you have fallen; repent, and do the works you did at first. If not, I will come to you and remove your lampstand from its place, unless you repent."

(Revelation 2:5)

James 4:4, which is written to Christians, indicates that God's acceptance of the believer is conditional. He asks: "You adulteresses, do you not know that friendship with the world is hostility toward God? Therefore whoever wishes to be a friend of the world makes himself an enemy of God" (NAS). James asserts that if our behaviors align with the agenda of this world we are in effect adulteresses. Apparently, James uses the feminine "adulteresses" to reflect the church's role as the bride of Christ. James teaches that this adulterous behavior makes us enemies of God.

It is troubling that contemporary evangelicals in asserting that our performance does not influence our relationship with God overlook this vast array of passages.

The Woman Taken in Adultery

Contemporary evangelicals frequently employ the story of the woman taken in adultery, found in John 8:3-11, to support their belief that God accepts people regardless of performance—unconditionally. This woman was taken from the very act of adultery and brought into the presence of Jesus. The passage gives no indication of remorse or repentance on her part and yet Jesus states, "Neither do I condemn you; go, and from now on sin no more." Therefore, this incident fits the contemporary evangelical template: Jesus displaying unconditional acceptance, which presumably will result in a change in her behavior. For that reason, many contemporary evangelicals reference this story in support of unconditional acceptance. In fact, it has been my experience that practically every extended discussion of God's unconditional love and acceptance references this passage for support.

Use of this story is problematic because almost every modern translation indicates in one way or another that this passage (John 7:53-8:11) is not included in the best manuscripts, which means that it is unlikely that it comprises inspired Scripture. Without getting too far into the weeds on the topic of questionable passages, the basic issue is that though we believe the original manuscripts of Scripture are without error, to our knowledge we have none of the original manuscripts. The manuscripts that we do have do not all agree. Most of the differences are minor and do not affect the message of Scripture. This passage probably comprises the most significant conflict found among the manuscripts.

Several different theories have emerged for determining which manuscripts contain the content of the original. The approach most widely accepted among Bible scholars supports the conclusion that this story was not included in the original manuscript and therefore is not actually part of the Bible.

Different versions convey this conclusion in different ways. For example, the English Standard Version (ESV) places this message in upper case letters in brackets right in the column of text: "THE EARLIEST MANUSCRIPTS DO NOT INCLUDE JOHN 7:53-8:11." They then include that section but enclose it with double brackets. The NIV includes in brackets in the column of text: "THE EARLIEST AND MOST RELIABLE MANUSCRIPTS AND OTHER ANCIENT WITNESSES DO NOT HAVE JOHN 7:53-8:11," but they also include this passage in the text. The majority of other recent versions of the New Testament use various approaches to convey the same message.

It is unfortunate that even though these versions assert that this passage is not in the most reliable manuscripts, which means that it is not part of the Bible, they nonetheless include it. Doing so is contradictory and creates confusion for God's people.

Practically every person who has received formal Bible training knows that the inspiration of this passage is highly improbable. Therefore, one would think that those seeking to validate unconditional acceptance would avoid this passage like the plague, not wanting to base their position on very shaky ground. Instead, they glom onto it like a drowning man grabbing a life preserver. In so doing they expose their own awareness of the lack of valid biblical support for their theory of unconditional acceptance.

Therefore, when you encounter contemporary evangelicals attempting to validate unconditional acceptance with the story of the woman taken in adultery, rather than viewing this approach as supporting their position, you will now recognize it as a testimony to the lack of support found in the genuine text of Scripture.

Legalism

The Contemporary Definition of Legalism

We have seen that contemporary evangelicals identify legalism as the enemy. This aversion to legalism flows out of their beliefs that we do not need to perform to please God. Based on this perspective, even the requirement to keep biblical commands is legalistic.

This perspective on legalism is linked to their contention that Christian living should always spring from desire and not obligation. Living based on obligation comprises an expression of performance. Consequently, Christian living should flow out of a "want to" motivation rather than be driven by an "ought to" motivation. Rules, laws, tell us what we ought to do. They embody obligation and the need to perform. Therefore, Christian living driven by rules fails to understand that God accepts us unconditionally.

Analysis

Scripture does not include the term "legalism." Therefore, technically we cannot establish a scriptural definition. Scripture condemns those seeking to bring New Testament believers back under the Old Testament law. For example, the book of

Does God Love and Accept Unconditionally?

Galatians opposes those requiring New Testament believers to be circumcised.

Further in the book, however, Paul asserts:

> For you were called to freedom, brothers. Only do not use your freedom as an opportunity for the flesh, but through love serve one another. For the whole law is fulfilled in one word: "You shall love your neighbor as yourself." (Galatians 5:13-14 ESV)

This verse indicates that while we are free from the Old Testament law, New Testament believers are obligated to keep the law of love. This, as already noted, includes all of the subsidiary commandments of the New Testament that flesh out the concept of agape. Murdering and stealing are contrary to love while generosity manifests it.

James expresses this perspective on Christian living as follows:

> But the one who looks into the perfect law, the law of liberty, and perseveres, being no hearer who forgets but a doer who acts, he will be
>
> blessed in his doing. If anyone thinks he is religious and does not bridle his tongue but deceives his heart, this person's religion is worthless. Religion that is pure and undefiled before God the Father is this: to visit orphans and widows in their affliction, and to keep oneself unstained from the world. (James 1:25-27 ESV)

We are free from the Old Testament law but are under the law of liberty, which calls us to love one another and love our enemies.

Paul states the case as follows:

> Owe no one anything, except to love each other, for the one who loves another has fulfilled the law. For the commandments, "You shall not commit adultery, You shall not murder, You shall not steal, You shall not covet," and any other

> commandment, are summed up in this word: "You
> shall love your neighbor as yourself." Love does no
> wrong to a neighbor; therefore love is the fulfilling
> of the law. (Romans 13:8-10 ESV)

Paul specifically states that we "owe" agape to others.

Preaching and teaching regarding our obligation to display loving behaviors does not comprise legalism but constitutes a necessary and edifying dimension of New Testament exhortation. Discouraging and even condemning it robs believers of an essential food group in the New Testament diet.

"Ought to" Passages

As already noted, contemporary evangelicals specifically assert that "ought to" motivation is legalistic, and that instead, we should maintain a Christian lifestyle because we "want to." However, the New Testament includes numerous passages that explicitly stipulate behaviors we "ought to" do. Here are a few:

- "If I then, your Lord and Teacher, have washed your feet, you also ought to wash one another's feet." (John 13:14)
- "Now we who are strong ought to bear the weaknesses of those without strength and not just please ourselves." (Romans 15:1 NASB)
- "So husbands ought also to love their own wives as their own bodies. He who loves his own wife loves himself." (Ephesians 5:28 NASB)
- "(W)hoever says he abides in him ought to walk in the same way in which he walked." (1 John 2:6)
- "By this we know love, that he laid down his life for us, and we ought to lay down our lives for the brothers." (1 John 3:16)
- "Beloved, if God so loved us, we also ought to love one another." (1 John 4:11)

These passages connote that an "ought to" motivation is biblical and valid. Just as the commands of Scripture make it evident that we are obligated to show agape, the "ought to" passages just quoted do likewise. Scripture makes it clear that we are obligated to perform.

Within Our Reach

Some contend that viewing God's love and acceptance as conditional places it out of the believer's reach because all of us sin. Therefore, they conclude that our inability to perform well enough to please God necessarily means that He must accept the believer unconditionally. Otherwise, no one could ever be acceptable to Him. Yancey expresses this line of reasoning in saying:

> The Christian life, I believe, does not primarily center on ethics or rules, but rather involves a new way of seeing. I escape the force of spiritual "gravity" when I begin to see myself as a sinner who cannot please God by any method of self-improvement or self-enlargement.[93]

Scripture, however, shows this position to be erroneous by asserting that the behavior of some of God's people has been pleasing to Him. For example, in Luke 1:5-6 we read,

> In the days of Herod, king of Judea, there was a priest named Zechariah, of the division of Abijah. And he had a wife from the daughters of Aaron, and her name was Elizabeth. And they were both righteous before God, walking blamelessly in all the commandments and statutes of the Lord.

Luke specifically indicates that he is not referring to imputed righteousness but behavioral righteousness—a blameless walk. Obviously, Zechariah and Elizabeth did not live perfectly. Therefore, this verse indicates that pleasing the Lord does not require perfection but a pattern of godly living.

Scripture describes Job in similar terms: "There was a man in the land of Uz whose name was Job, and that man was blameless and upright, one who feared God and turned away from evil." (Job 1:1) Scripture cites other persons who also maintained lives pleasing to the Lord.

We all fail many times, and for this reason God makes the provision for forgiveness as we confess and forsake our sins. Our objective should be to live with a clear conscience before God in the present moment. This we can do. In light of God's provision of the Holy Spirit and other resources, we will never find ourselves in a situation in which sin is inescapable. We never need to sin. Rather, sin is a choice, unfortunately one that all of us make many times. But when we do sin, God has provided a means of forgiveness and restoration of fellowship that is always accessible to us. Therefore, at any given moment our lives can be pleasing to God, and that should be our continuous objective. Consequently, though God's love and acceptance are conditional, God has placed the means of meeting those conditions within our reach. We can live in such a way that we enjoy God's approval, as did Zechariah, Elizabeth, and Job.

Chapter 3: Selfishness and Agape Production

As noted in the previous chapter, the concept of unconditional love and acceptance and its companion teachings related to performance and legalism are blatantly unscriptural.
This chapter addresses the damages they are inflicting.

License to Live Selfishly

As the title of this book suggests, the primary negative impact of the evangelical embrace of unconditional love and acceptance resides in its extending to believers a license to live selfishly. In earlier chapters we observed that unconditional acceptance eradicates all restrictions on the receiving individual, even allowing him to harm others with the assurance that he will receive continued love and acceptance.

This acceptance of the individual regardless of his lifestyle is especially potent since evangelicals assert that it emanates from God. It is one thing for a therapist or parent to extend unconditional love and acceptance, but it is even more impactful when the individual is given the assurance of God's love and acceptance regardless of his lifestyle. If a believer is cohabiting, unconditional acceptance by a therapist or friend still leaves him to deal with his conscience. Their acceptance might marginally blunt his guilt, but assurance of God's unconditional acceptance would go much further in quieting his conscience.

The assurance that he does not need to perform to please God further frees him to live as he pleases. Likewise, the perspective that he can do nothing to make God love him more or less also assigns him the latitude to follow his desires wherever they might lead. The teaching that living based on rules constitutes legalism also lifts any restrictions on his behavior. Responding to any pangs of conscience or disapproval by others only consigns him to a rules-based Christianity that does not acknowledge biblical grace or his freedom in Christ. The assurance that when God looks on him, He does not see his behavior but only the righteousness of Christ assuages any remaining guilt feelings. These concepts license him to maintain any lifestyle he chooses. This freedom unleashes his fallen nature to exert its tendency toward selfishness.

Difficulty of Biblical Agape Production

This arrangement may not be too devastating if the life of agape, the one to which God called us, came naturally and easily. However, we observed earlier that producing agape constitutes a highly challenging task, requiring the intentional management of our lives. Though we are joined by the Holy Spirit in pursuing that objective, God has left us with a major part of the action, and meeting our responsibilities requires our total focus, commitment, and energies.

We find this truth underscored throughout the New Testament. For example, the apostle Paul likens the Christian life to a boxing match.

> Every athlete exercises self-control in all things.
> They do it to receive a perishable wreath, but we an
> imperishable. So I do not run aimlessly; I do not box
> as one beating the air. But I discipline my body and
> keep it under control, lest after preaching to others I
> myself should be disqualified. (1 Corinthians 9:25-27).

In this passage, Paul confesses his need to exercise discipline to keep his body in subjection. Paul admonished Timothy to "Fight the good fight of the faith" (1 Timothy 6:12). The word "fight" in this passage translates the Greek word from which we get our English word "agony." Paul is challenging Timothy to discipline himself to live biblically even when doing so becomes agonizing, a task requiring discipline and endurance.

Agape production comprises a battle that believers all too often find themselves losing. Galatians recounts Paul calling out Peter, point-man for the church, for unbiblical behavior. Of the seven churches described in Revelation 2-3, only two had a sterling record, with three getting mixed reviews, and the remaining two doing poorly. A serious look at our own lives quickly divulges the presence of failures and the accompanying realization that agape production constitutes a battle.

In light of the struggle to produce agape, issuing the believer a license to live selfishly makes the prospect of agape production far less probable. Assuring the believer that God will be just as pleased with him if he runs the race, enduring the agony, or sits in the stands, gorging himself with French fries and Coke, increases the likelihood of his taking the latter option.

The Contemporary Evangelical Solution

Contemporary evangelicals join Carl Rogers in the belief that the experience of unconditional acceptance will produce the desire to opt for productive behaviors. Evangelicals make an even stronger case by teaching that unconditional love and acceptance emanates from God.

The first problem with this position, a lethal one, resides in the fact that, as noted in the previous chapter, the teaching of God's unconditional love and acceptance is contrary to Scripture.

A second problem is found in all of the passages of Scripture such as 1 Corinthians 9:25-27, quoted above, that describe living the Christian life as a struggle. If we could soar above the struggle merely by experiencing God's unconditional love and acceptance, Scripture would not include such passages. Instead, it is full of them. This spiritual "easy button" is not found anywhere in Scripture. Rather, Scripture extends to us the call to engage in the battle with the world, the flesh, and the devil, enduring hardness as good soldiers of Jesus Christ. At times we may feel like producing agape, but often doing so entails making difficult decisions and exercising substantial discipline to implement those decisions.

A third problem in the contemporary evangelical teaching that we should maintain a biblical lifestyle not because we ought to but because we want to is found in those times when we do not feel like behaving biblically. If we should only function in response to a *want to* motivation, what should the believer do when he does not *want to* act biblically? That describes my situation many times a day. Those situations leave us with two options: we can follow our desires toward selfish behaviors or discipline ourselves to produce agape. Contemporary evangelicals reject both of those options. They would not advocate sinful living, but they view motivation by rules, "ought to" living, as a return to legalism. This quandary leaves many contemporary evangelicals confused. Even worse, in the face of confusion, they tend to choose the easier option, to follow their desires toward selfish behaviors.

These and other problems reveal that the contemporary evangelical approach to agape production does not work. Producing agape only when we want to will often lead to selfish living. In fact, the next chapter describes some selfish trends that are being produced as a result of these contemporary perspectives on Christian living.

Killing Agape Production with a Two-Edged Sword

The contemporary evangelical perspective licenses believers to live selfishly, vastly reducing agape production. This error, however, represents only half of the problem. It kills agape production with a double-edged sword by also discouraging the biblical approach of exercising discipline in order to follow the commands of Scripture, insisting that doing so is legalistic and counterproductive. This licensing to live selfishly while warning against disciplined Christian living comprises a formula for disaster. Let me illustrate.

National intelligence discovered that a foreign nation has imprisoned 10,000 Christians, is treating them cruelly, and plans to execute them next year. The White House tasks the Department of Defense with forming an infantry division specifically designed to attack this country and rescue these prisoners. The Secretary of the Army assigns General Jones to command this division, designated as the Agape Division because of its unique rescue mission. He is instructed to devote six months to forming and training the unit in preparation for their mission and then await the command to attack the enemy and rescue the beleaguered Christians. The Department of Defense calculates that this division of 15,000 men supplied with all of the latest equipment is more than adequate to achieve its objective.

General Jones, having been influenced by our culture, has adopted a contemporary approach to training troops. He believes that requiring rigorous disciplines and training programs produces an inferior soldier. He is convinced, instead, that unconditionally accepting soldiers will motivate them to train and fight optimality, not because they have to, out of obligation, but because they want to. He does not want soldiers to feel that they must perform to please him, but rather he wants them to know that he is pleased with them regardless of their performance. He believes that as they experience his unconditional acceptance, they will spontaneously train and fight at optimal levels.

Consequently, upon taking command he called a meeting of all the division officers to announce his new policies, which he wants them to convey to the troops. He indicates that he accepts the soldiers of the division unconditionally and that consequently they do not need to perform to please him. He instructs these officers to reflect the same attitude in their dealings with their troops. Their performance should not in any way affect the attitude of these officers toward them or the way they treat these soldiers.

In addition, he accentuates his belief that requiring soldiers to follow rules creates a counterproductive response, prompting them to train and fight out of obligation, because they have to and not because they want to. This legalistic approach, General Jones explains, has created the inferior armies of the past and must be avoided at all costs. He explains that it is fine for officers to offer teaching and training, but they must explain to the troops that they should only participate if they want to and not out of a sense of obligation. Likewise, these officers can explain military standards of conduct to the troops, but the soldiers should only follow these guidelines if they want to and not because they feel an obligation to obey them.

His officers strongly urged Gen. Jones to reconsider, arguing that without conditions of acceptance, stipulating requirements for training and rules of conduct, the soldiers would not spontaneously exercise the necessary discipline to train adequately and would even fall into chaotic, destructive behaviors. In addition, when the time came for battle, this unconditional acceptance and abandonment of rules may prompt many of the soldiers to decide not to fight. In response, Gen. Jones insisted, "Military experts now realize that the soldier who is accepted unconditionally and not corrupted by legalistic demands will spontaneously behave as he should."

Initially, the soldiers were delighted by the new approach and thought Gen. Jones was the best division commander ever. Many soldiers responded enthusiastically to the new policies and trained even harder. In addition, as word got out, recruitment increased dramatically. From all indications, the new Army was a smashing success.

In time, however, many soldiers stopped engaging in physical fitness. Also, attendance precipitously declined at training sessions teaching use of weapons and military tactics. The reality that they were not obligated to follow military disciplines soon set in, and most stopped saluting officers and even started to ignore their instructions, now given in the form of suggestions. It did not take long for chaos to set in.

The day of reckoning came six months and two weeks later when the Secretary of Defense issued orders to the Agape Division to assault the nation imprisoning the Christians and rescue them. Many of the soldiers ignored the order to embark for the journey, indicating that they were enjoying their leisurely life on the Army post. Those who did agree to go had no clue regarding how to function as a military unit or even use their weapons. Neither were they physically fit to fight. Their incapacity to fight effectively and failure to follow orders left them as easy targets for the enemy. Soon the Agape Division was overrun, many were killed, and others taken prisoner. They failed in achieving their agape mission, and ultimately the imprisoned Christians were executed. This division failed to display agape toward these Christians, toward the President and the Department of Defense that issued their orders, and to the nation that had fed them and clothed them for six months and counted on them to accomplish their mission. They even failed to display agape toward one another by failing to meet responsibilities that would have protected their fellow soldiers in combat.

The contemporary evangelical church, which advocates a similar approach, is likewise experiencing defeat as evidenced by its powerlessness to inhibit progressive advances despite its God-given resources to do so.

On the positive side, the contemporary evangelical Christian enjoys three advantages that the benighted Agape Division did not have.

A major advantage resides in the believers' possession of the Holy Spirit. Despite the confusion caused by erroneous input, He nonetheless encourages them toward agape production. For example, while the contemporary evangelical church may teach that God accepts us unconditionally, the Holy Spirit still prompts us to produce agape and convicts us when we live selfishly. As already emphasized, the Holy Spirit serves as a helper but does not do the work for us. Therefore, though His ministry does not totally undo the negative effects of licensing selfishness, it does serve to lessen its impact.

Another advantage enjoyed by the contemporary evangelical resides in the church's commitment to the truth of Scripture. It preaches and teaches Scripture and encourages its people to read it. While the contemporary evangelical church tends to cherry-pick passages, shying away from commands to live righteously and passages dealing with God's chastening those practicing sinful behavior, the teaching of Scripture nonetheless produces a positive impact. Also, some churches encourage their people to read through Scripture, which exposes them to the full range of truth.

In addition, many leaders who are the greatest advocates of contemporary evangelical beliefs nonetheless preach excellent sermons and produce other materials that advocate some elements of a biblical approach to Christian living that reflects the traditional perspective. They seem not to notice the inconsistency.

One other benefit that contemporary evangelical believers enjoy resides in common sense. Believers tend to realize that just as they need to exercise discipline in every other area of life in order to succeed, they must discipline themselves in pursuing spiritual objectives. At times they may not feel like displaying agape toward their spouses, but common sense tells them that they should and that they need to discipline themselves to do so.

The bottom line is that the double-edged sword of propagating an erroneous theory and discouraging the employment of a biblical approach is weakening the contemporary evangelical church. Though the ministry of the Holy Spirit, the input of Scripture, and common sense rescue it from total disaster, it nonetheless is falling substantially short of maximum agape production.

What evidences of damage do we find in the contemporary evangelical community resulting from its licensing selfishness rather than promoting agape production? The chapter ahead describes those outcomes.

Chapter 4: Damages Inflicted by Unconditional Acceptance

Our examination of the concepts adopted by contemporary evangelicals has revealed that they are not compatible with Scripture and give license to living selfishly rather than producing agape. This finding leaves us to wonder how much harm this embrace of error has inflicted on the evangelical community. Let's assess the damages.

Condoning the Viewing of Nudity

One practical area in which the contemporary evangelical message of unconditional acceptance and the resulting license to live selfishly displays its influence resides in the acceptance of viewing movies that include nudity.

On December 26, 2013, Alissa Wilkinson wrote a review on the movie *The Wolf of Wall Street* for *Christianity Today*.[94] This movie contains the full spectrum of ungodly behavior, but the review especially indicates that it includes substantial nudity. Wilkinson nonetheless gave the movie 3 ½ stars out of four for factors such as artistic value. She indicates that most of her readers will not feel comfortable watching this movie but left the door open for those who might.

This review elicited a response from Trevin Wax of *The Gospel Coalition* entitled "Evangelicals and Hollywood Muck,"[95] in which he pondered, "My question is this: at what point do we consider a film irredeemable, or at least unwatchable? At what point do we say it is wrong to participate in certain forms of entertainment?" The fact that by some counts *The Wolf of Wall Street* contains 22 sex scenes in part prompted his concern.

Wax's article led to an article by Wilkinson in response: "Why We Review R-Rated Films: You're a neighbor before you're a consumer",[96] which prompted a second response from Wax: "Christians and Movies: Are We Contextualizing or Compromising?"[97]

These interchanges might be summarized as follows: Wilkinson apparently has no problem with nudity in movies as long as it is not gratuitous but instead conveys art, enables us to understand who we are, portrays real-life (as does the Bible), faithfully conveys the intended message, or enables us to minister to our neighbor by entering into his culture. Trevin Wax expressed concern that the eroticism of movies such as *The Wolf of Wall Street* may be so blatant as to override any artistry and redeeming message. This led him to wonder where to draw the line, but he found no answer, in part being restrained by fear of regressing toward his legalistic childhood. As observed earlier, contemporary evangelicals view establishing any standards of behavior is legalistic.

Consequently, Wax is not able to stipulate viewing nudity in movies as a place to draw a line. Though I found Wax's search for a standard commendable, his inability to identify one, even related to an issue as obviously troublesome as nudity, was disappointing. Yet the contemporary evangelical perspective on legalism requires this conclusion.

Because these two evangelical sources are highly visible and authoritative, we have good reason to believe that they represent the majority position of contemporary evangelical Christianity. Consequently, this discussion reveals that the contemporary evangelical emphasis on God's unconditional acceptance and its related concern over legalism has brought us to the point where viewing nude women in movies is legitimate or at least should not be labeled as wrong.

Another indicator of the broad evangelical acceptance of nudity in movies is found in the minimal objections to this trend. Since it is endorsed by very visible evangelical sources, if strong beliefs did exist to the contrary, we would expect that open challenges to these endorsements would be quick and vehement in their appearance. I will discuss later some negative responses to this trend that have been forthcoming. These, however, comprise a minority position, with the general evangelical culture trending toward acceptance of viewing nudity in movies.

This trend leads us to ask whether the justification for viewing of nudity is valid.

- Does labeling something as art justify a practice? No doubt many strippers would view what they do as art, and perhaps rightly so. After all, if dancing is art, why would doing it undressed not be? Is it okay to go to strip clubs as long as the believer is there to appreciate the art? Legitimizing practices by identifying them as art does not serve as a valid criterion.

- Does the fact that movies portray real life as we find it in the Bible legitimize it? Can we really believe that the Bible's mention that David and Bathsheba committed adultery is morally equivalent to watching adultery performed in a movie? I do not believe that anyone can make that case in sincerity and honesty.

- Does loving my neighbor by relating to him culturally require my viewing films with nudity? Of the full spectrum of contemporary culture, must I include that piece in my repertoire in order to understand and relate to him? I do not believe anyone can honestly make that case either.

How do we know if a believer should engage in a particular practice? Throughout this book we have emphasized that God calls us to produce maximum agape: love for God and neighbor. What conclusions might we draw by using that criterion to assess viewing of nudity in movies?

Let's begin our assessment by first considering the impact on the viewer.

- How many males can assert with honesty that they have the capacity to view a nude actress, who in most cases would be an extremely attractive woman, without lusting, especially when, as is usually the case, she is depicted in a sensuous context? I believe that almost all honest males would confess their inability to do so. This conclusion leads us to ask whether watching such movies shows love toward Christ who commanded men not to look at a woman with lust.

- God had a good reason for giving men the command not to lust. Doing so is not healthy emotionally, relationally, or behaviorally but instead promotes problems in all these areas. Therefore, watching nudity in films is not loving because of its negative impact on the viewer and others harmed as a result.

- I suspect that most wives whose husbands view a nude woman in a movie, especially an attractive one in a sensuous setting, would feel jealousy and betrayal, though they may not express those feelings. Therefore, in many cases, this practice is unloving to wives.

- In this area, most men might be considered "weaker brothers," not able to view nudity in movies exclusively as art appreciation. Therefore, even if I can maintain a pure heart while engaging in this practice, doing so is unloving toward the other 99% of males who may be tempted to indulge by my example.

- The impact on the behaviors of unmarried couples resulting from this practice seems to be self-evident. In most cases,

doing so would erode morals, the foundational element of agape. Critics may contend that
if the movie portrays a negative outcome to promiscuous sex, viewing it may enhance the morality of viewers. This position exposes naivety regarding human nature. The high levels of emotional arousal created by nudity would make a far stronger impression than some underlying moral message. In addition, in most cases, nudity in movies is not used to promote a positive moral message.

Another consideration related to whether viewing nudity in movies maximizes agape has to do with the women who expose themselves in this form of entertainment.

- Phillip Holmes in a *Desiring God* article summarizes John Piper's critique of the issue of viewing movies with nudity in seven points, many of which I believe are quite compelling.[98] From my perspective, the most incontrovertible one is related to concern for the women who expose themselves. Regarding this behavior, Piper observes that you cannot fake nudity. A movie can portray a robbery or murder that is not an actual robbery or murder, but the nudity is real. A human being is degrading herself by exposing her body to every man who chooses to look. Whether she realizes that this is degrading makes no difference. Therefore, viewing a movie in which she does so implicates the viewer in her self-degradation, a practice that is selfish rather than loving.

- Piper also asks how many husbands or parents would want their wife or daughter to appear nude in a movie, exposed for the whole world to see? Therefore, watching someone else's wife or daughter expose herself is unloving to husbands and parents.

We must also ask whether this practice maximizes agape in the societal sense.

- When women expose themselves to millions of men, how does that affect our cultural fiber? How does it impact the sexual development of children who are exposed to it—and more have access to it than we would like to think? How is it affecting the morals of teenagers? What influence does it have on moral behaviors of dating couples? How is it affecting fidelity in marriages? What does it do to individual and national character? Any reasonable assessment must conclude that this practice is having a negative impact in all these areas, contributing substantially to our cultural decline. Therefore, viewing movies with nudity does not comprise an expression of agape toward society in general, but selfishness.

- How does this practice affect the spiritual life of believers? Does it present a spiritual environment in which the Holy Spirit is free to work? Scripture and experience seem to indicate that this is not the case. It seems likely that the individual is less inclined to spend time in Scripture or prayer after watching a movie containing nudity. If this practice has a negative impact on our spiritual life, it is detracting from our capacity to show agape to God and others.

I have devoted substantial space to this narrow slice of contemporary evangelical culture because it is more helpful to consider in detail a specific issue rather than paint with a broad brush. In addition, this does not entail an area where evangelicals are trying but failing, but a practice being broadly accepted as legitimate.

Yet another reason for highlighting acceptance of viewing nudity in movies is the likelihood of this practice encouraging other negative trends within evangelical society. We know that use of pornography runs rampant in the church. Here are some 2014 statistics for Christian men between 18-30 years old: (1) 77% look at pornography at least monthly; (2) 36% view pornography at least daily; (3) 32% admit being addicted to pornography (and another 12% think they may be). The statistics for middle-aged men are not much better.[99] I wonder if the acceptance of viewing nudity in movies is not serving as a "gateway drug" to pornography. It is easy to see how it could.

First, it could whet the appetite of many males for more. Also, it would make it easy for a person to rationalize that if evangelicals believe that watching nudity in movies is okay, why is it worse to watch it on the Internet?

We might also sense concern for evangelical women. An article dealing with the attraction of evangelical women to *Fifty Shades of Grey* by E.L. James reports,

> Indeed, Christians, usually resolute on the dangers of porn, are big fans of James' explicit and allegedly profane sexual tales, as Barna Group researchers discovered in a survey last year. The evangelical Christian research group reported that "there is no difference between the percentage of Christians who have read Fifty Shades of Grey and the percentage of all Americans who have read the book."[100]

It seems that viewing nudity in movies has also served as a "gateway drug" for women, making them more vulnerable to pornography and other forms of erotic input. Therefore, it is unloving to these women to participate in drawing them into this moral black hole.

Likewise, one wonders whether the burgeoning tendency among girls and young women toward sexting, taking and sending nude selfies, is not motivated at least in part by the acceptance of viewing nudity in movies. If female nudity is legitimate in that context, why not for them? Taking down these cultural guardrails and consequently increasing the vulnerability of these girls does not display agape, especially when we realize that they may be engaging in a practice that could embarrass and hurt them for the rest of their lives. Imagine if their future husband, children, neighbors, or coworkers discovered those pictures.

This discussion reveals a deeper issue. The embrace of unconditional acceptance and the consequent war against legalism has prompted a greater concern over whether the believer is free to engage in a practice than whether it produces agape. We have become absorbed with whether viewing nudity is acceptable as opposed to whether it produces agape toward God and in our ministry to others. Contemporary evangelicals also display this orientation regarding other lifestyle issues. In consequence, we have adopted an orientation diametrically opposed to the one to which God has called us. If producing agape were the focus, it would become immediately evident that viewing nudity in movies does not comprise the most promising means of reaching that objective.

Consequently, evangelicals, instead of functioning as a restraining force against the full menu of seduction being served by the sexual revolution, are participating in promiscuous entertainment as well as cohabitation, infidelity, divorce, and other manifestations of sexual promiscuity. We will consistently be on the losing side of the culture war as long as our orientation and objectives focus on what we perceive as our freedoms rather than on agape production.

Sexual Promiscuity as a Marker of Societal Collapse

Why is national and evangelical decline in the sexual arena so significant? An article by Ed Vitagliano entitled "The morally heroic and the rescue of culture" provides an answer. He cites two secular studies, a 1934 book entitled *Sex and Culture*, by British anthropologist J. D. Unwin and a 1956 study by Pitirim A. Sorokin, founder of the sociology department at Harvard University, entitled *The American Sex Revolution*. Both studies indicate that the sexual wellness of societies determines their success as a whole.[101]

Vitagliano summarizes:

> Both Unwin and Sorokin saw a common factor in every such decaying society: changing attitudes and actions regarding monogamy in marriage.
>
> Strong cultures always upheld monogamy in marriage and resisted a loosening of mores regarding sex outside it. However, when the people turned away from this view of sex and marriage, they always began the process of decline.

> In effect, cultures always experienced something akin to our own sexual revolution as a catalyst to the decay process....

> Unwin said the culture "that tolerates sexual anarchy is slowly but surely debilitating itself, impairing its collective health and endangering its very survival."

Another finding of these studies cited by Vitagliano is that sexual promiscuity in a society signals the existence of wider spread societal chaos:

> Sexual laxness becomes a manifestation of a broader and deeper problem—a growing love of pleasure and self-indulgence. In order to enjoy life's pleasures, self-discipline is cast aside and decay sets in, much like a once strong and fast athlete who has retired to a luxurious but sedentary lifestyle loses the "edge" that once resulted in excellence.

Likewise, the sexual chaos in the evangelical community described above signals broader evangelical cultural decay. One article reveals:

> The findings in numerous national polls conducted by highly respected pollsters like The Gallup Organization and The Barna Group are simply shocking. "Gallup and Barna," laments evangelical theologian Michael Horton, "hand us survey after survey demonstrating that evangelical Christians are as likely to embrace lifestyles every bit as hedonistic, materialistic, self-centered, and sexually immoral as the world in general." Divorce is more common among "born-again" Christians than in the general American population. Only 6 percent of evangelicals tithe. White evangelicals are the most likely people to object to neighbors of another race. Josh McDowell has pointed out that the sexual promiscuity of evangelical youth is only a little less outrageous than that of their nonevangelical peers.[102]

This extensive article cites many statistics over a broad range of societal issues, and virtually all show evangelicals trending with secular decline. Moreover, the trajectory among evangelicals is moving in the wrong direction. George Barna concludes: "Every day, the church is becoming more like the world it allegedly seeks to change."[103]

An article by Fr. John Zuhlsdorf also analyzes Unwin's massive study, citing its finding that a sexually promiscuous society collapses within three generations. The study specifically indicates that this collapse includes the disappearance of rational thinking.[104] Examples abound of the abandonment of rational thinking in contemporary American society. For example, the practice by most universities of censoring conservative positions and even providing trigger warnings and safe spaces to prevent student exposure to them displays the closing down of rational inquiry at the highest levels of academia. An article by John Zmirak noting the implication of this study for our nation observes, "We're on that third generation right now. And we're right on schedule."[105]

The evidence reveals that our nation has been brought to the brink of ruin by sexual promiscuity. Nonetheless. the contemporary evangelical church rather than countering this trend is contributing to the problem. This situation is especially troubling.

Though it is difficult to establish cause-and-effect in studies, particularly those dealing with social trends, one can see the rational connection between the secular and evangelical license to live selfishly and these trends, especially in light of our natural human inclination toward perverse behaviors. If God is just as pleased with me regardless of what I watch, how much I eat, or how I treat other people, my desires will pull me toward selfish choices rather than those producing agape.

Vitagliano's article also contains some good news, suggesting a path to recovery from our current cultural slide. That is the focus of the next chapter.

SECTION FIVE
RECOVERING AND WINNING

This section describes how contemporary evangelicals can stop the licensing of selfishness and regain the strength to function as salt and light in our dark and evil world. It also outlines a plan that the evangelical church, with restored health and strength, can employ to win the culture war. I am convinced that winning is well within our reach. Achieving it only requires the restoration of evangelical spiritual health and an effective plan.

Chapter 1: Road to Recovery

The Good News

Ed Vitagliano's article cited in the previous chapter includes an encouraging finding. He reports:

> Historically, there were always some within a culture that resisted the initiation of sexual revolution, and these people hindered the corruption process.

> While neither Unwin nor Sorokin was religious, both argued from their research that a decaying society might be saved—but only if there remained within it a stratum of citizens who were willing to hold to the culture's moral traditions.
>
> Sorokin explained that, as the ideas and consequences of a sexual revolution become evident, the members of this moral resistance "become more religious, morally heroic and sexually continent in the periods of disorders and great calamities."
>
> If they remained committed to sexual restraint and monogamous marriage; and if these counter-revolutionaries did not themselves succumb to the rising tide of immorality; "the process of decline may be halted," Sorokin said, and the society "may regain its mental and moral sanity; may halt the dangerous drift through complete deterioration."

This article informs us that a minority can save a society. These findings correspond to the teaching of Jesus that a minority of Christians functioning as salt and light can exercise a preservative force in society. The evangelical church in America could serve as a mighty army comprising that minority if it would purge itself of the debilitating secular beliefs described in this book and recommit itself to a biblical orientation.

What would this restorative process require?

Production of Agape

This question returns us to the beginning of the book, which asserted that agape production comprises the power source that transforms individuals and societies. But as noted throughout this book, agape production is challenging, requiring that we work and fight to produce it. The contemporary evangelical teaching that gives license to selfishness is preventing the church from functioning as that minority that can restore our culture.

How can the evangelical community revitalize its agape production? Doing so requires four initiatives.

Submission to God's Authority

Managing our resources to maximize agape production begins by acknowledging the authority of God. Without awareness of His authority and commands, we tend to make selfish rather than agape-producing choices. Imagine a company where no one was in charge—no authority existed. Very quickly chaos would set in and production would tank. The reason is that humans require authority to function optimally. This reality applies to our agape production. Acknowledgment of God's authority comprises its driving force.

As our society has rejected the existence of God and consequently His authority, selfishness with all of its malevolent byproducts has increased exponentially. Human beings tend only to produce agape consistently in response to God's authority.

However, belief in the existence of God but asserting that God loves and accepts unconditionally eradicates His authority. Therefore, the road back to agape production requires purging the evangelical community of the error of God's unconditional love and acceptance and the reinstatement of God's authority. Consider the significant role of authority embodied in the great commission:

> Go therefore and make disciples of all nations, baptizing them in the name of the Father and of the Son and of the Holy Spirit, teaching them to observe all that I have commanded you. And behold, I am with you always, to the end of the age." (Matthew 28:19-20)

This passage, Christ's parting words to us recorded in Matthew, commands us to make disciples and indicates that discipleship must include an emphasis on the authority of Christ. He insists that we observe everything that He commanded.

Countless other New Testament passages demonstrate that submission to the authority of Christ comprises an essential ingredient of New Testament living. Even the often-repeated acknowledgment that Jesus is Lord embodies this truth. In Luke 6:46 Jesus asks the penetrating question, "Why do you call me 'Lord, Lord,' and not do what I tell you?" Jesus does not just want us to view the designation "Lord" as an honorary title. Rather, He calls us to take His authority seriously. Only as we acknowledge His authority will we maximize agape production.

Embracing God's Truth

Authority only wields influence when we identify and respond to the instructions of the one holding that authority. We can claim the government has authority, but if we are unaware of or ignore all the laws of the country, we are in effect functioning as if that authority does not exist. Likewise, we can acknowledge the authority of God in theory but ignore it in reality by not accurately and fully embracing and implementing the truth of Scripture. Acknowledging God's authority but ignoring His instructions allows for selfish living.

Numerous passages cited in this book demonstrate that many contemporary evangelical concepts are blatantly unbiblical. Many passages show them to be so. Adoption of these unbiblical concepts reveals that contemporary evangelicals are not taking Scripture seriously in these areas, instead allowing culture to shape their perspective on the Christian life.

Assigning ultimate authority to Scripture and ascertaining the truth that it embodies requires that evangelicals read Scripture again for the first time. That is, they need to set aside all their preconceived notions about what it says, especially ones interjected by our culture, and allow it to speak for itself.

Likewise, it is essential to read and take seriously all of it. Evangelicals must put aside their tendency to cherry-pick and instead take as authoritative those passages that do not fit the contemporary evangelical template. If they were not essential to our spiritual well-being, the Holy Spirit would not have included them in Scripture. Consequently, eliminating them from our spiritual diet skews our understanding of God and His program, thus reducing agape production.

Throughout this book, I have referenced the New Testament almost exclusively. I have done so to avoid the accusation that my concerns consist of legalistic Old Testament concepts that have now been replaced by the New Testament teaching on grace.

However, the Old Testament has value. Contemporary evangelicals for the most part tend to write it off as not having application to us. It is fascinating how many evangelicals often recite Jeremiah 29:11, "For I know the plans I have for you, declares the LORD, plans for welfare and not for evil, to give you a future and a hope." Yet they are quick to ignore other Old Testament teachings, viewing them as having no application to their lives.

However, 2 Timothy 3:16-17 teaches that "All Scripture is breathed out by God and profitable for teaching, for reproof, for correction, and for training in righteousness, that the man of God may be complete, equipped for every good work." During the times when the New Testament was written, for the most part the only Scripture the church had was the Old Testament. Therefore, most references to Scripture in the New Testament are referring to the Old Testament. This fact indicates that the writers of the New Testament viewed the Old Testament as applicable and valuable for New Testament believers.

Though many Old Testament teachings do not apply to us as we live under the New Covenant, we can nonetheless learn much from the principles they convey. For example, many of God's people have succeeded in life in large measure by applying the wisdom they learned from the Book of Proverbs. The Old Testament teaches us much about the nature of God. Though God's program has changed, God has not. Many of the errors currently embraced by contemporary evangelicals might have been avoided had they given the Old Testament portrayal of God appropriate consideration.

Restoration of evangelical vitality requires taking all of Scripture seriously and formulating our understanding of the Christian life from it. We must allow it, and not culture, to inform us regarding our relationship with the Lord and how to live the Christian life. The evangelical church will only maximize agape production when it responds to the authority of God transmitted through the truth of Scripture.

Re-engaging with the truth of Scripture will require that individual believers continuously read and ingest all of Scripture, that preachers and teachers expose their congregations to the full range of biblical truth, and that evangelical writers and bloggers confirm all spiritual truth to the minds and hearts of their readers. Only by so doing will the evangelical church develop the spiritual vitality necessary to save America.

Responding to God's Motivation

The primary characteristic of a humanistic system resides in its belief that human beings possess within themselves a drive for goodness and appropriate behavior. They claim that humans behave badly because some blockage exists that impedes this positive human drive from expressing itself. Different humanistic systems provide us with diverse theories regarding the nature of this blockage that hinders optimal human functioning.

This humanistic template eliminates the need for motivation for humans to behave well and function optimally. Since humans possess this innate drive toward goodness, they do not require motivation to act appropriately. They only need to have the blockage removed.

We observed this theory at work in subjectivism as described by Norman Mailer. He contended that the blockage was the authority imposed on the individual by society, and if that authority were removed and individuals were granted autonomy, they then would spontaneously behave productively. We see the same perspective manifested in elements of our society today that want to defund the police, believing that somehow in the absence of their authority people will behave legally. They are convinced that humans do not need the motivation to act properly imposed by law enforcement.

Carl Rogers contended that the blockage was conditional acceptance, and that the person accepted unconditionally would spontaneously act appropriately. The Rogerian therapist is careful not to include in therapy motivational language such as suggesting how a person ought to live or why his current behavior was irrational and destructive.

Communism, though not viewed as a humanistic theory, follows a similar pattern, teaching that the worker possesses a natural inclination toward production. Repressive capitalism, however, creates a blockage that prevents him from producing optimally. If the worker were freed from this oppression and provided with an income from the state according to his needs, he would produce optimally without being motivated by reward for higher production.

The contemporary evangelical approach to agape production also follows this template. It contends that legalism, the belief that we must perform to please God, comprises the blockage to agape production. Embracing God's unconditional acceptance removes that blockage. Therefore, performing in order to please God and to receive his blessing and reward constitute unbiblical motivations. They believe if this legalistic blockage is removed, then the believer will spontaneously display agape.

Their position eradications biblical motivation. God is equally as pleased with the believer whether he disciplines himself to get up early to read Scripture or decides to sleep in. God will not chasten him for viewing pornography or bless him for resisting the temptation. He will enjoy God's favor just the same if he uses his money to buy a more expensive car he does not need or gives the money to support a missionary. Consequently, he has no real motivation to make harder agape decisions. God is just as pleased if he opts for the easier selfish ones. In other words, it removes motivations to produce agape.

Therefore, the contemporary evangelical perspective on motivation follows the humanistic and communistic template. Its perspective on motivation in effect comprises spiritual communism.

All of those systems have shown themselves to be abject failures. We have observed the devastating impact that subjectivism has had on our society. Likewise, the outcomes of Rogers' experiment revealed the specious nature of his theory. Communism and socialism have failed at every attempt. Socialism's ruination of the once-prosperous Venezuela provides just the most recent manifestation that its theory is seriously flawed. All these failures reveal that humans require motivation to function optimally. In its absence, they underproduce at unsustainable levels.

One might wonder whether believers need motivation. After all, we possess the Holy Spirit who inclines us toward agape producing behaviors. Maybe this template doesn't work for humanists and communists, but perhaps it works in the Christian context.

This position is shown to be erroneous on two counts. We find our need for motivation displayed both in our own performance and also in the teaching of Scripture.

A superficial analysis reveals that even believers do better when motivated. I find losing weight difficult. I have been struggling to lose five pounds across the past month without success. Had someone offered me a million dollars to lose five pounds, would I have lost it? You better believe I would have—and an extra five just to make sure. If motivation results in reaching other goals, no doubt it contributes to agape production also.

We find this truth reflected in Scripture. Many passages of Scripture describe various motivations God provides to believers. For example, Jesus gave us the parable of the minas in Luke 19. Each servant was given one mina with which to earn a profit. Jesus describes the response to the servant earning 10 minas as follows:

> The first came before him, saying, 'Lord, your mina has made ten minas more.' And he said to him, 'Well done, good servant! Because you have been faithful in a very little, you shall have authority over ten cities.' (Luke 19:16-17)

The servant that produced five minas received five cities, a good reward but a lesser amount commensurate with his productivity. The one that made no profit was rebuked for his laziness. Here we find Jesus motivating the reader by teaching that those who work hardest will receive the greatest reward.

Peter offers both positive and negative motivation in 1 Peter 3:8-12:

> Finally, all of you, have unity of mind, sympathy, brotherly love, a tender heart, and a humble mind. Do not repay evil for evil or reviling for reviling, but on the contrary, bless, for to this you were called, that you may obtain a blessing. For "Whoever desires to love life and see good days, let him keep his tongue from evil and his lips from speaking deceit; let him turn away from evil and do good; let him seek peace and pursue it. For the eyes of the Lord are on the righteous, and his ears are open to their prayer. But the face of the Lord is against those who do evil."

Therefore, instead of teaching that performance is not necessary to please God, evangelicals must emphasize just the opposite, that production of agape pleases God and results in enjoying His fellowship and receiving His blessing and reward. As with the authors of Scripture, it is essential for Christian leaders to challenge believers to pursue God's blessings and avoid His chastening. Biblical motivations presented in sermons, blog posts, and books will result in the production of sufficient quantities of agape to engender spiritual health and empower us to engage effectively in the culture war.

Developing Discipline

Because agape production is challenging, requiring focus, intention, and hard work, generating it demands not only motivation but also discipline. We might acknowledge the authority of God, clearly understand the guidance of His Word, and be motivated to achieve it. If, however, we lack discipline, our good intentions regarding the production of agape will not be achieved. This is especially the case if we lack the discipline to overcome our selfish inclinations. Consequently, the restoration of evangelical vitality and optimal agape production requires an evangelical culture that accentuates the value of discipline—the development of internal strength.

We develop discipline by choosing harder but better behaviors over easier, inferior ones. Scripture teaches that we develop character by making biblical choices when confronted with challenging circumstances. "Not only that, but we rejoice in our sufferings, knowing that suffering produces endurance, and endurance produces character, and character produces hope." (Romans 5:3-4) Paul is not suggesting that suffering per se produces endurance and character. People can respond toward suffering with despondency or anger, which does not result in endurance but further erosion of character. Paul is speaking of developing discipline and character through responding to suffering with faith and courage.

Historically in our nation, parents, schools, and the church engaged in character development. The evangelical community has historically been a bulwark for the development of discipline and character in our nation. The teaching of unconditional acceptance and the assertion that we do not need to perform to please God is undermining its functioning in that role. Many contemporary trends reveal that evangelicals are desperately lacking in the area of discipline. For example, the incapacity of vast numbers of evangelical men to stand up to the temptations of pornography demonstrates this erosion of discipline.

To remedy the situation, it is essential that Christian parents teach their children scriptural mandates and train them in the application of these virtues. Pastors and other evangelical leaders need to consistently challenge their flock with the need for discipline, character development, and endurance. Whenever possible, parents must place their children in an educational environment that encourages discipline. Where that is not possible, they must place special emphasis on character development in the home.

Though teaching the principles of Scripture provides the necessary foundation for character development, teaching is not sufficient. Parents and others must also train young people in the *application* of these principles, which will develop discipline and strength of character. Knowing about physical fitness is important. Going to the gym is essential. Above all else, completing the Seal training course requires discipline. This is also true of the Christian soldier in his fight against the world, the flesh, and the devil.

This lack of discipline and the related strength of character is responsible to a great degree for the domination of evangelicals by the left. It is impossible to effectively engage in the culture war without the development of discipline. In fact, historically, discipline has comprised a prime characteristic of the military. Only a highly disciplined soldier possesses the strength to effectively engage in combat.

Agape against the Darkness

In the Christian classic, *Hiding Place*, Corrie Ten Boom relates the efforts of her family in the Netherlands during World War II to help Jewish people escape Nazi capture. Ultimately the Nazis caught and imprisoned this family. It is challenging to observe the strength they exhibited resulting in their display of agape in the midst of some of the most difficult circumstances imaginable.

Corey's father, Casper Ten Boom, was a godly, wise, and humble man who owned a watch repair shop. He was in his 80s and feeble when the Germans apprehended the family and interrogated them to determine their fate. The chief interrogator, spotting this elderly and feeble man and displaying an unusual moment of compassion said, "That old man!.... Did he have to be arrested?" He called Casper up to his desk and said, "I'd like to send you home, old fellow.... "I'll take your word that you won't cause any more trouble."[106] Corrie recounts:

> I could not see Father's face, only the erect carriage of his shoulders and the halo of white hair above them. But I heard his answer.

> "If I go home today," he said evenly and clearly, "tomorrow I will open my door again to any man in need who knocks."

> The amiability drained from the other man's face. "Get back in line!" he shouted. "Schnell! This court will tolerate no more delays!"[107]

In so stating, Casper Ten Boom pronounced his own death sentence, dying in prison not many days later. However, his proclamation of dignity and strength, this glorious expression of agape, pierced the walls of that dark and evil Nazi court and comes down to us today as an example of the agape, courage, and power God calls us to display as the darkness and evil of the left press in on us.

That power to stand against the darkness, however, did not come merely as an inspiration of the moment. It emanated from deep roots. The book reveals that Casper Ten Boom drank deeply and regularly from Scripture, which motivated him to apply its guidance to every dimension of his life. This formed within him a godly personality secured by a disciplined character. When confronted by the forces of evil, he stood like a tree planted by the rivers of water that brought forth fruit in its season.

American evangelicals comprise only a minority of the population. However, through responsiveness to the authority of Christ, through ingesting and taking seriously the guidance of Scripture, through its motivation to develop godly personalities, and through the resulting discipline, empowered by the Holy Spirit they can comprise a formidable force capable of winning the culture war. Regarding capitulation to the culture, Francis Schaeffer implored, "In the name of the Lord Jesus Christ, may our children and grandchildren not say that such can be said about us." To this I would add, may history instead record that in this dark hour in American history, following the example of Casper Ten Boom, we displayed an abundance of agape sufficient to stand against and defeat the culture of evil confronting us and make America great again.

Chapter 2: Winning

Do We Love Enough

Genuine love drives people to overcome evil and produce just, safe, and prosperous outcomes. The same pertains to the evangelical church in the United States today. Love for unborn babies about to be murdered, for our children who are drowning in a society characterized by moral depravity, and for our grandchildren destined for an even worse plight, should impel us to rise above inaction or inadequate action to develop and implement a plan that will take back our nation from the left and restore justice, rationality, and righteousness. Likewise, love for our neighbors who are increasingly immersed by the left in a culture that will destroy their humanity and degrade their relationships should drive us to provide them with a better environment. Only the church possesses the capacity to do that. Above all, our love for the Lord should drive us to obey His command to function as salt and light in order to shape our culture so that He is honored and His Word exercises influence.

We are not there now. We must face that reality. The evangelical church in America has developed no plan and is executing no plan to defeat the left and retake our nation. This assertion is not meant to minimize the efforts of those brave evangelical warriors on the front lines who are engaged in the battle and sacrificing much. Those efforts notwithstanding, it is essential for us to face the reality that the evangelical church has not committed itself to win the culture war and restore righteousness in America.

The evangelical church for the most part has delegated the task of protecting us from the left to parachurch organizations. These committed organizations serve to keep us informed, let our voice be heard in the public square, and organize boycotts. However, as separate entities, their impact can only be marginal and therefore their objectives realistically can only be limited. They have neither the power nor the reach to think in terms of winning the culture war. The best we can hope for from them is keeping the wolves away from the church door, and that objective may even be an overreach considering the many weapons wielded by the left. We are grateful for their doing what they can, but our expectations must be realistic.

The proof of the pudding regarding their success reveals itself in the continued advance of the left. We are clearly on the losing side, and the enemy is closing in on us with every passing day. This reality became increasingly clear recently when Justice Neil Gorsuch led the way on a 6-3 majority declaring that the 1964 Civil Rights Act's ban on employment discrimination based on "sex" also covers lesbian, gay, bisexual, and transgender workers. This ruling opens the door wide for progressive advancement of their agenda and their assaults against evangelicals.

The current ineffective response of the church reveals that we lack sufficient agape for unborn babies, our children, our grandchildren, our neighbors, and our nation to take substantive action to rescue them. Though this may seem like a harsh assertion, the facts make it inescapable.

Some evangelicals may respond that engagement in this fight is not the church's business. I addressed that issue in the opening chapter. Let me briefly reiterate here that if we believe that rescuing innocent unborn babies, and even those having been born, from murder is not our business, we might need to reconsider what business we are in. How does agape not include the rescue of our most helpless and most innocent neighbors? This same logic pertains to our engagement in the fight against many other aspects of the evil agenda of the left. The command of Christ to love our neighbor enlists us as combatants in this war whether we like it or not. In that sense, His church does not consist of a volunteer army. Rather, Christ has drafted us all.

Some may respond that evangelicals are doing what we can. They may contend that the enemy is too strong. Again, at the outset of the book, I cataloged the resources available to us and noted that the early church with far fewer resources, numbers, and freedom transformed the Roman Empire.

It is not true that we lack the resources. We don't. The truth is that we are not sufficiently engaged in the battle and effectively using those resources. This chapter contends that if we would fully engage, we could triumph over the left. We are failing to do so for two reasons. First, the infection by secular culture described in the previous sections of this book has left us failing to produce sufficient agape to fight effectively. We must first resolve that problem as described in the chapter above. The second reason we are losing resides in our failure to develop and implement a plan for winning.

Planning to Win

What would such a plan look like? That is the topic for the remainder of this chapter. It lists six actions that would assure evangelical victory in the culture war.

#1: Corporate Prayer

Some may think that prayer constitutes a strange and ineffective strategy for launching a counterattack in the culture war. However, prayer comprises the greatest resource the church possesses. It is essential for discerning God's guidance. It is essential for unleashing God's power to fight the battle confronting us. Without it, the rest of our strategy will lack spiritual guidance and power, resulting in defeat.

We profess to believe that God hears and answers our prayers. God's people are being assaulted by a powerful and evil enemy, and we are on the brink of defeat. In similar circumstances Jehoshaphat called on God, God heard his prayer, and brought about the enemy's defeat. Likewise today, prayer must be the first response in engaging the left.

In light of this spiritual reality, it is perplexing that during these days when the enemy is coming up over the church walls, attacking bakers and photographers and other Christian businesses, that during most Sunday morning services in most churches no mention is even made of these assaults in the morning prayer. Likewise, prayer is seldom made for our brothers and sisters in other countries who are being beheaded, raped, and enslaved.

One reason for this omission stems from the short shrift prayer receives in general in Sunday morning services in the overwhelming majority of evangelical churches. This omission is especially egregious since the morning worship service comprises the main gathering of the church. We leave ample time for worship (singing), the sermon, announcements, and the offering, but little time—perhaps no more than a minute or two—is allotted for prayer. And most of that time is consumed with concern for our own church body to the exclusion of prayer regarding the decline of our nation and the plight of fellow Christians around the globe.

This arrangement conflicts with instructions of the Apostle Paul:

> First of all, then, I urge that supplications, prayers, intercessions, and thanksgivings be made for all people, for kings and all who are in high positions, that we may lead a peaceful and quiet life, godly and dignified in every way. (1 Timothy 2:1-2)

Most commentators agree that Paul is referring to prayer during the worship service. He is instructing that we give it first priority—not last—in our primary gathering of the week. Despite this unequivocal exhortation to pray, beginning with the pressing words "First of all," seldom if ever is this glaring, prevailing, ubiquitous deficiency acknowledged. I have heard fine pastors give urgent calls for prayer while being unwilling to devote substantive time to prayer in the morning worship service. This arrangement communicates to the congregation that the church leadership does not genuinely believe in prayer's significance and effectiveness. Their actions speak louder than their words.

Most prayer meetings, which even in many large churches are attended by only a handful of people, consist primarily of Bible studies and prayer requests, with minimal time dedicated to actual prayer, revealing that we do not believe our own teaching about prayer. Since prayer is our greatest resource, it is not surprising that we are losing the culture war.

Given this glaring blind spot—neglecting the powerful resource of prayer, a church strategy must begin by rearranging the morning worship service to devote a significant portion of time, such as half an hour, to prayer. It is ironic how foreign such an approach seems to us while Scripture conveys that it was the norm for the early church—the church that transformed the Roman Empire. We find a further irony in the fact that the shrinking American church persists in its corporate prayerlessness while the church in other countries that assigns priority to corporate prayer is growing.

On the positive side, a church that purges itself of secular ideology and engages in the culture war beginning with prayer can expect victory. God is still answering prayer, still unleashing His power on behalf of believers. The same God who transformed sinful cultures through prayer in the past is still at work today.

#2: Church on God's Terms

Most contemporary evangelical churches offer church on your terms. You can come and go as you please, join or not join, participate or not participate, serve or not serve, and pretty much live how you want. This approach to church reflects the influence of the subjectivist attitude that the individual has a right to do his own thing. It also manifests the teaching of unconditional acceptance, which views the individual as okay regardless of how he chooses to do church.

Church on our terms, however, differs from church on God's terms, and failure to do it His way is not working. Rather, it leaves the church with an inadequate foundation for developing strong Christians who will produce optimal agape and can fight effectively in the culture war.

Who's in and Who's Not

One manifestation of church on our terms is an unidentified church body. No one knows for sure who's in and who's not. Joe, Sally, and their children have attended for years but have never joined. Because they attend somewhat regularly, the church lists them in its directory. Is this family part of the church body or not? Who knows? This is the way the system is currently set up, and no one seems to have a problem with it or asks whether this is God's design.

Scripture suggests a different model by holding leadership accountable for its constituents.

> Obey your leaders and submit to them, for they are keeping watch over your souls, as those who will have to give an account. Let them do this with joy and not with groaning, for that would be of no advantage to you. (Hebrews 13:17)

This passage asserts that Christian leaders will give an account to God for those under their charge. Church on our terms does not support this accountability. Leadership can meet this biblical responsibility only by identifying specifically who belongs.

This would require that churches clearly define their membership—individuals for whom the leadership is responsible to give an account to God. Visitors are welcome, but the identity of the flock should remain clear to leadership and the congregation.

We noted that all relationships require conditions for meaning, structure, and functioning. This includes the church. The failure of contemporary evangelical churches to identify and enforce these conditions has left the church lacking biblical meaning, biblical structure, and a biblical basis for functioning. Establishing biblical conditions for church membership will provide the basis for the organization, supervision, care, and training of those in the church body.

Structure

Many churches have a small group ministry, but participation is usually voluntary. Imagine if each church, with its constituency now clearly defined, would assign every member to a group that reflects where they are on their spiritual journey. They would place new believers in discipleship groups and assign those already discipled to groups that would help them identify their spiritual gifts and develop those capacities. Other groups would have more specialized functions such as in-depth Bible study, helping those with drug or alcohol problems, preparation for marriage, parenting, or dealing with personal finances. Children and youth would have specialized small groups, perhaps focused on systematic development of biblical knowledge and character building.

The church would train group leaders. These leaders would both teach and have oversight responsibility for those in their groups, caring for the well-being of each individual and family and providing a resource for those facing challenges. In turn, these small group leaders would report to an overseer, serving as a structure that enabled church leadership to give an account for every individual belonging to the body regardless of the size of the church.

Imagine how much healthier church members would be and how much stronger the church as a whole would be as a result of utilizing this organizational structure. This structure would lend itself to maximum production of agape within the lives of individuals, families, and the church body. It would also provide structure and training for engagement in the culture war.

Perhaps the immediate reaction to the structure described above might be: "You've got to be kidding. That will never happen." It is interesting that every other major institution—government, business, education—mandates structure. Why? Because that's how things get done. So why then should the church not do likewise?

It might be argued that a systematic approach to church organization, teaching, and training is not doable in our current society. I pastored a church that employed the type of structure described above. This was not my doing, but I inherited it from the excellent work of the previous pastoral staff. They initiated a program in which every new member was assigned to a small group with a "caring couple" that met with and shepherded them. Each elder had the oversight of several "caring couples." The "caring couples" reported to the elders regarding the welfare of those in their group. This resulted in the ability of the elders to provide oversight to every individual belonging to the church, which they did effectively. Such an arrangement is possible in contemporary America, and it is quite effective.

The structure and training described above would enable every church to function as an outpost in the culture war, with well-equipped soldiers and the organization necessary to mobilize them. The structured local church would provide the basic building block for the evangelical army. Only as evangelicals adopt church on God's terms by developing a functioning organizational structure will it possess the capacity to win the culture war.

#3: Unity

It is scandalous that the left manifest unity, bringing together elements as diverse as homosexuals, feminists, and Muslims, while Christians, whom Christ called to unity, cannot join together in fighting the culture war—or in doing much else for that matter. Something is seriously wrong with that picture.

We can only effectively engage in the culture war through unified action. This unity must have churches and denominations as its centerpiece. Though many individuals and parachurch organizations fight hard in the culture war, victory requires engagement by the church per se—the bodies that meet on Sunday morning for worship. It is essential for them to join in unified action in order to win the culture war. Unity comprises a major principle of war. Fragmented efforts will incur defeat.

Recently a school board decided that biological boys would be permitted in girls' shower rooms. One girl was in tears at the prospect of having to undress while boys watched. This policy is outrageous and morally destructive on many counts. A typical evangelical response to this type of situation is to write articles about it and maybe to appear at the board meeting to protest. These responses are ineffective in producing change.

However, if the churches in the area united and organized, showed up by the thousands at the meeting and assured schoolboard members that this policy would result in even greater demonstrations at the school and their being voted out at the next election, they could stop this insanity in its tracks. We can only achieve victory with unity.

I cannot stress this point strongly enough. Unified we can win. Without unity we cannot. It is that simple. For example, conservatives constantly bemoan censorship by social media, and for good reason. The Internet even more than the mainstream media comprises the primary channel for communication in contemporary America, and from every indication this trend will only increase. If social media and Google are free to censor, they can severely restrict our capacity for getting out our message while freely promoting their own. In so doing they can control public opinion, elections, and most other critical aspects of contemporary American life.

Almost every time conservatives complain about censorship, someone reminds them that these outlets are privately owned, and they have a right to decide which items they will carry and which they will not. Some argue that they are functioning as a monopoly and therefore need government control. Whatever the outcome of that debate, we can count on the fact that as long as the left owns social media, it will exercise censorship as it does with the mainstream media and other outlets. If we were unified, however, we could initiate our own social media that would be good enough and powerful enough to compete with current outlets and attract the general public. Without unity, we are at the mercy of the left.

Most of the other challenges currently confronting us could be won if we were unified. Seeking to take action without unity usually results in evangelicals being picked off one at a time, being marginalized, and losing their jobs. We can only combat today's "cancel culture" with a unified response.

Prior to the Revolutionary War, colonists began to establish Committees of Correspondence, which spawned unification among the colonies. They recognized that without unity, the colonies would be at the mercy of England. The unity they created laid the foundation for America's victory in the Revolutionary War, our nation, and the resulting freedom.

Likewise, today, evangelical denominations, churches, parachurch organizations, and other evangelical entities need to work toward a form of unity that will enable us to fight the tyranny of the left. I believe that the left's greatest fear is a unified evangelical opponent. They know that if we were united, we could win the culture war, but as long as we remain fragmented, they can dominate us. The "Moral Majority," which contributed substantially to the election of Pres. Reagan, displayed the power of unified evangelicals.

Unified action could be achieved through the establishment of a social action center, an organization that would provide leadership and coordinate the influence of all evangelical denominations, churches, and parachurch organizations in fighting the culture war. Though all involvement would be voluntary, effectiveness would require a high degree of participation.

Figures vary widely regarding the percentage of Americans who are committed evangelicals. These differences result primarily from differing definitions of the term "evangelical." However, it seems that about 10% of Americans are seriously committed to Christ, with a substantially larger percentage that identify as Christians but reflect a lesser level of commitment. Consequently, an American population of about 330 million suggests the presence of about 33 million committed evangelicals.

However, if evangelicals were unified and were taking meaningful action, many more of those who identify as Christians would join them. Many Millennials are looking for a cause worth living and dying for, which the contemporary evangelical church is currently not providing. I am convinced that if evangelical Millennials saw the church actively and meaningfully engaging in the culture war, instead of dropping out they would be at the forefront of the battle.

An effectively functioning social action center would also inspire renewed participation by men. Contemporary churches are losing men because their feelings-oriented, unconditionally-accepting message is a turnoff for many men. Evangelical churches replacing that message with one promoting character and strength would again attract men. As the unified church effectively engaged in the culture war, they would show up ready to participate in the fight.

#4: Leadership

The development and operation of a social action center would require a skilled and motivated leader. The wrong leader, especially one stuck in the contemporary evangelical unconditional acceptance mode or one who is not sufficiently aggressive, would make this entire initiative a liability rather than an asset. It would result in squandering resources without gaining victories, giving evangelicals a sense that they were achieving something when they were not.

At the outset of the Civil War, the North was losing because its generals would not fight, a source of consternation for President Lincoln. Likewise, the teaching of unconditional acceptance has sapped Christians of the fighting spirit necessary for engaging in the culture war. It is essential to appoint a leader who is willing to engage aggressively in the culture war.

The Apostle Paul's confrontation with Elymas provides us with a model for taking on the fight with evil.

> But Elymas the sorcerer (for so his name is translated) withstood them, seeking to turn the proconsul away from the faith. Then Saul, who also is called Paul, filled with the Holy Spirit, looked intently at him and said, "O full of all deceit and all fraud, you son of the devil, you enemy of all righteousness, will you not cease perverting the straight ways of the Lord? And now, indeed, the hand of the Lord is upon you, and you shall be blind, not seeing the sun for a time." And immediately a dark mist fell on him, and he went around seeking someone to lead him by the hand. (Acts 13:8-11 NKJV)

This verbal and spiritual assault did not comprise a fleshly outburst, but rather this passage tells us that Paul spoke these words in response to being filled with the Holy Spirit.

Contemporary evangelicals would condemn this type of response as harsh and unloving. I believe, though, that we need this type of conviction and strength in presenting our position. The left displays far greater strength in advancing its agenda than do most contemporary evangelicals. Winning the culture war requires a leader with the strength and willingness to confront evil as did Jesus in cleansing the Temple and Paul in the passage above.

#5: Expertise

Waging war includes planning and strategy, which requires a high level of expertise. The social action center would need to identify and utilize personnel for its staff with savvy in areas such as an acute understanding of Scripture, politics, marketing, communications, use of social media, management, finances, education, public relations, etc. God has blessed the church with these skilled people. With unity and an effective leader, these skilled people would be eager to employ their expertise in fighting the culture war.

The LGTBQ community successfully advanced its agenda by employing the strategy presented in the book *After the Ball – How America will conquer its fear and hatred of Gays in the 90s*, by Marshall Kirk and Hunter Madsen.[108] Kirk was a researcher in neuropsychiatry and Madsen earned a doctorate in politics from Harvard and worked in advertising on Madison Avenue.[109] Their effectiveness demonstrates the benefit of high levels of expertise in developing a strategy. Christians must find and utilize people with that level of skill in order to succeed.

#6: Strategies for Winning

Evangelicals empowered by prayer, with churches configured according to God's design, unified, guided by an effective leader, and advised by a staff with wide-ranging expertise would comprise a formidable fighting force. The one remaining essential element would reside in the formulation of an effective strategy aimed at winning. With a social action center, an effective leader, and a team of experts, the development of a winning strategy would be well within our reach.

Though the team of experts would be capable of developing a strategy far beyond anything I could devise, I mention the following ideas just to demonstrate the possibilities.

Evangelistic Engagement

The social action center could coordinate a national campaign to create awareness among Americans of some facet of the gospel message, e.g. "Your life on earth will end—and then what?" For a month the message that someday everyone has an appointment with death could be communicated in various creative forms through radio and television advertising, social media, billboards, etc. This message would be carefully crafted, using the best marketing techniques. Pastors could plan messages related to this theme. Churches could train people in how to effectively engage in conversations related to this theme.

This coordinated effort would flood the nation with a singular message that those in secular society might even begin to look for and discuss. This sort of coordinated campaign would give both motivation and opportunity for Christians to engage friends in conversation. It could shape our culture by arousing a focus on an undeniable spiritual truth.

That month might conclude by scheduling evangelistic campaigns throughout the nation. By the end of the month, people would be more inclined to attend one of those rallies or watch it on television or the Internet. Above all, this saturation with a potent message may prepare them to be responsive.

Political Engagement

The social action center could wield substantial influence in national, state, and local elections, in many cases determining the outcome. Its potential becomes evident when we consider that most elections are decided by just a few percentage points.

The social action center could provide information that would help Christians make informed choices.

More organized churches and strategies employed by the social action center would encourage a far greater percentage of evangelicals to vote, making a huge difference in outcomes. In the 2016 presidential election, approximately 61% of evangelicals turned out.[110] Some estimate that 81% of evangelicals voted for Pres. Trump, a major factor in securing his election.[111] If the initiatives above resulted in a 91% turnout, as opposed to 61%, this result would make a huge impact on election outcomes.

Cultural Engagement

The social action center could help shape the culture by guiding and encouraging conservative entertainment. In a recent article, Patrick Courrielche highlighted the need for conservatives to develop their own entertainment industry by asserting:

> It's not just that Tinseltown will never respect Middle America. Hollywood's gatekeepers will never allow the Right to enter its gilded gates to tell our stories. And this is important because as the late great Andrew Breitbart often said, "Politics is downstream of culture." Storytelling is one of the most influential forms of human communication. It has the power to change minds. Just a few years ago, one movie – *Gosnell* – singlehandedly altered my position on abortion. That is the power of good storytelling. The Left knows this, and they will never give the Right a seat at the table because of it. [112]

Some progress has already been made in producing conservative entertainment, but often its impact is marginalized by the limited exposure given by theaters. Unity and strategy could go a long way in rectifying these types of problems and increasing the conservative impact on the culture.

The social action center could also influence culture by organizing boycotts of companies that were supporting immoral causes. The American Family Association has done some effective work using boycotts, but the social action center, mobilizing a united evangelical community, would exercise far greater influence.

This strategy could counter the "cancel culture" that the left uses to punish individuals and companies supporting Christian values. One wonders if the left would have been able to force Brandon Eich out of Mozilla if evangelicals had possessed this type of organization. Without it the left can destroy a man such as Brandon Eich, putting every other CEO and prominent person on notice that they are vulnerable to a similar demise if they display even the least opposition to its agenda. Therefore, a united evangelical presence is essential.

Rallies

As an element of its strategy, the social action center could organize rallies for believers in many areas of the country to provide encouragement and spiritual input to evangelicals as well as a means of evangelistic outreach. Imagine the impact if in even moderate-sized population centers, evangelicals could fill stadiums to overflowing with only a modest amount of advertising. This could be achieved by the social action center's coordination of evangelical efforts through well-organized churches and social media. Such rallies could enhance unity and provide a sense of solidarity, consequently energizing participants and attracting others.

Demonstrations

Demonstrations comprise a more drastic strategy, but one legitimized in some instances by the evil aggression of the left, the immorality of their objectives, and the resulting destruction to our nation.

The recent Supreme Court decision supporting people congregating at casinos in Nevada but banning their right to assemble in churches has been viewed by many as a judicial outrage. This pandering to the left without concern of any retribution from evangelicals encourages this type of travesty. I am convinced that Supreme Court justices would not be so cavalier in ruling against churches if confronted with the threat of mass demonstrations by evangelicals that exposed this sort of judicial bias.

Our leadership would need wisdom to determine which battles we should fight, how, and when. Carefully chosen and well-executed implementation of this strategy would serve to significantly advance the fight against the left and re-establish a Christian culture in our nation.

The First Step

If the contemporary evangelical church is willing to take the first step listed above, engagement in corporate prayer, the other items will fall into place resulting in victory. The need is not for a special prayer initiative, concerts of prayer, or even prayer meetings, though these are good and helpful. The need is for churches to carve out a significant segment of the primary church service—for example, half an hour—for this purpose. Churches need to shorten other activities, lengthen the service, or do whatever is needed to make this happen.

Willingness to take this first essential step, one within the reach of every church, one that costs no money, will provide the power and momentum for the rest of the strategy and the resulting victory. There is no question whether the evangelical church can take back America. It can. Whether it will all depends on the evangelical church's willingness to take this first step. The question is whether we possess sufficient agape: love for our country, our children, our grandchildren, and our neighbors, to take the initiative.

Hour of Decision

Sinkable

On the tenth day of April 1912, the *Titanic* left Southampton, England, on her maiden voyage to New York City. So confident were her builders that she was unsinkable that they included only enough lifeboats to accommodate half of her 2,200 passengers and crew, and those were only intended to pick up passengers of other ships that may have sunk. When at 11:40 PM on April 14 she hit an iceberg and began to take on water, activities on the ship continued as usual and without anxiety. Elizabeth Shutes, a survivor, reported being assured that everything was okay and consequently took no action to prepare to abandon the ship. It was not until she overheard an officer state, "We can keep the water out for a while," that she knew danger was serious and imminent.[113]

Sometime within the two hours and 40 minutes between the *Titanic's* collision with the iceberg and its sinking beneath the waters the awful reality of impending disaster set in. During that time men took their wives and children to lifeboats, knowing that they were seeing them for the last time. Within the next few hours, 1522 passengers and crew perished in the icy waters.

Most Americans convey a belief that our nation is unsinkable. Recently, a talk show host after lamenting our societal decline concluded, "There will always be an America," connoting that while our nation may not continue to enjoy present levels of freedom and affluence, it will survive in its current form. This same conviction that America is unsinkable reflects itself in evangelical attitudes as evidenced by a lack of definitive actions. Though in the 1960s we hit an iceberg and are taking on water, we will not sink but only float a little lower in the water.

The ultimate tragedy of the *Titanic* resides in the prospects that she could have been saved. Joseph M. Greely wrote an article describing various actions that likely would have prevented its sinking, or at least kept it afloat long enough to rescue all of the passengers.[114] The *Carpathia*, the ship that rescued *Titanic* passengers from her lifeboats, arrived less than two hours after the *Titanic* sank. Greely calculates that appropriate action would have kept the *Titanic* afloat at least that long. He believes that the inactivity of the captain, who seemed to be in shock, ultimately resulted in it sinking. How tragic if the demise of the

United States resulted from the inactivity of evangelical Christians, who have within their grasp the capacity to save it.

Our Options

The culture that progressives are imposing on our society promotes selfishness and drains agape. Their agenda has shriveled America to a vestige of its previous greatness and is threatening our way of life and very existence. Only bold, aggressive, definitive action by the evangelical church will save it.

This country was founded predominantly by Christians and with a Christian cultural orientation. That cultural orientation brought this nation success. Therefore, fighting for and demanding a return to that orientation, represents the rational and rightful realignment of America. The enemies of Christianity are the intruders in this nation, and we are its rightful heirs. We must divest ourselves of the attitude that somehow this is their country and we are outsiders, having to settle for whatever crumbs they are willing to drop from their table. Instead, we must rid this nation of their evil influence, reestablishing the God of the Bible, the Creator referenced in the Declaration of Independence, as the God in whom we trust and whose authority we acknowledge.

If you believe that some of the courses of action described above are too aggressive, I would invite you to consider the actions taken by the left. In an America unquestionably founded with a Christian cultural orientation, they have criminalized prayer and Bible reading in schools, legalized the murder of unborn babies, changed the definition of marriage to include homosexual relationships, and given sexual preference legal priority over religious conviction, just to reiterate a few of their victories.

They have not been timid in advancing their agenda to transform a country that is not theirs while we have been on the defensive, weak, and tentative in our response, managing only to react to their initiatives, positioning ourselves never to *take* ground but at best not to lose too much. They have lied, cheated, and employed other immoral tactics to achieve their aims.

Unless the American evangelical church goes on the offensive, unless it develops an agenda of its own that seeks to aggressively take back this country, we will allow the wicked forces currently dominating this country to drag it to its demise—and us and our children with it.

Our only options are to defeat them or to be destroyed by them. As our nation fought for its very existence during World War II, General Douglas MacArthur eloquently framed the reality confronting us in these terms: "From the Far East I send you one single thought, one sole idea—written in red on every beachhead from Australia to Tokyo—There is no substitute for victory!" That same reality confronts the church today in our war against America's internal enemies.

Soon it will be too late, but the door of opportunity is still cracked open sufficiently for God's people to achieve victory if we are willing to fight. If we pray that God provides us with the will, courage, and wisdom to do so, if we commit ourselves to defeat those who have imposed an ugly, godless, agape-devouring culture on our nation, if instead we move as a mighty army to restore our life-giving, agape-producing Christian culture to its rightful place, then the future of this nation will be that expressed by Francis Scott Key in the final verse of our National Anthem:

> Then conquer we must,
> when our cause it is just,
> And this be our motto:
> "In God is our trust."
> And the star-spangled banner in triumph shall wave
> O'er the land of the free and the home of the brave.

Endnotes

1 https://www.dailywire.com/news/walsh-the-confused-andpointless-rage-of-an-entitled-generation?itm_source=parselyapi?utm_source=cnemail&utm_mediu m=email&utm_content=072820 -news&utm_campaign=position7

2 Horowitz, David. Blitz: Trump Will Smash the Left and Win. West Palm Beach, Florida: Humanix Books, 2020, p. 193.

3 https://www.cbsnews.com/news/france-less-work-more-time-off/

4 https://nypost.com/2020/06/03/nba-voice-grant-napear-opensup-on-all-lives-matter-firing/

5 https://www.nationalreview.com/2020/06/welcome-toamericas-cultural-revolution/

6 https://mail.google.com/mail/u/0/#inbox/FMfcgxwJWrgFTbfPQmrJrPHwnVZsPsfp

7 Hart, David Bentley. Atheist Delusions: The Christian Revolution and Its Fashionable Enemies. New Haven & London: Yale University Press, 2009, p. xi.

8 http://nchfp.uga.edu/publications/nchfp/lit_rev/cure_smoke _cure.ht ml

9 http://www.dailymail.co.uk/sciencetech/article-3181290/Howfar-away-candle-Raging-debate-finally-extinguished-thanks-studyputs-distance-just-1-6-miles.html

10 https://en.wikipedia.org/wiki/Christianity_in_the_United_Sta tes#:~:te xt =Christianity%20is%20the%20most%20adhered, lower%20than%2078%25%20in%

11 http://www.patheos.com/blogs/blackwhiteandgray/2013/03/h owmany-americans-are-evangelical-christians-born-again-christians/

12 Ibid.

[13] https://www.barna.org/barna-update/article/13-culture/111survey-explores-who-qualifies-as-an-evangelical#.VcXmsSb49SE

[14] http://inthepastlane.com/today-in-history-histdykmosquitoes-and-the-battle-of-yorktown/

[15] Schaeffer, Francis A. The Great Evangelical Disaster. Westchester, Illinois: Crossway Books, 1984, pp. 63-65.

[16] https://en.wikiquote.org/wiki/Andrew_Breitbart

[17] https://scienceuprising.com/

[18] https://news.gallup.com/poll/268205/americans-believegod.aspx

[19] http://www.nydailynews.com/entertainment/tvmovies/americans-spend-34-hours-week-watching-tv-nielsennumbers-article-1.1162285

[20] Postman, Neil. Amusing Ourselves to Death: Public Discourse in the Age of Show Business. Penguin Books, 1985, p. 71.

[21] Ibid. p. 73.

[22] Ibid. p. 78.

[23] Bork, Robert H. Slouching Towards Gomorrah: Modern Liberalism and American Decline. New York: Regan Books, 1996, p. 263.

[24] Ibid. p. 264.

[25] Ibid.

[26] Searle, John R. "Rationality and Realism, What is at Stake?" Daedalius, Fall 1993, p. 55.

[27] Barone, Michael. Hard America, Soft America: Competition vs. Coddling and the Battle for the Nation's Future. New York: Crown Forum, 2004, p. 12.

[28] Ibid. p. 13.

[29] https://en.wikipedia.org/wiki/Herbert_Marcuse

Endnotes

30 http://www.merriam-webster.com/dictionary/subjectivism

31 Norman Mailer. "The White Negro," in Existentialism, ed. Robert C. Solomon. New York: Modern Library, 1974, pp. 331-332.

32 Mailer, p. 334.

33 Mailer, p. 335.

34 Whitehead, p. 66-67.

35 Eskridge, Larry (2013-05-31). God's Forever Family: The Jesus People Movement in America. Oxford University Press USA [Kindle Edition, p. 30].

36 Whitehead, p. 5.

37 Whitehead, pp. 66-68.

38 Whitehead, p. 33.

39 It has been asserted that Dostoevsky did not say this. The following link, however, makes the case that he did. http://infidels.org/library/modern/andrei_volkov/dostoevsky.html

40 Diana West. The Death of the Grown-Up. New York: St. Martin's Griffin, 2007, pp. 1-2.

41 Ibid. p. 4.

42 Solomon, p. 335-336.

43 William Bennett. "Does Honor Have a Future," Imprimis, December 1998, p. 1.

44 https://en.wikipedia.org/wiki/Norman_Mailer

45 http://nypost.com/2014/02/07/obamacare-freeing-the-joblocked-poets/

46 Kilpatrick, William Kirk. Christianity Today: "Therapy for the Masses," November 8, 1985, p. 21.

47 Carl R. Rogers. On Becoming a Person: Boston: Houghton, Mifflin Company, 1961, p. 163.

48 Ibid. Kilpatrick.

[49] http://www.christianpost.com/news/mozilla-ceo-on-gaymarriage-row-i-keep-my-personal-beliefs-out-of-the-office-117217/

[50] Letter from William C. Coulson dated November 25, 1997, 1.

[51] William Coulson. "We overcame their traditions, we overcame their faith." The Latin Mass. Harrison, NY, Special Edition, 13.

[52] Ibid. p. 14.

[53] Ibid. p. 14.

[54] Ibid.

[55] Ibid. p. 13.

[56] Ibid.

[57] Ibid.

[58] Ibid.

[59] Ibid. p. 14.

[60] Ibid.

[61] Ibid.

[62] Ibid.

[63] Ibid. pp. 14-15.

[64] Ibid. p. 15.

[65] Ibid. p. 15.

[66] Kugelmann, Robert. "An Encounter between Psychology and Religion: Humanistic Psychology and the Immaculate Heart of Mary." Journal of the History of the Behavioral Sciences, vol. 41(4), 347-365, Fall 2005.

[67] Letter from William C. Coulson dated November 25, 1997, p. 1.

[68] Carl R. Rogers (quoted from a speech at the 1981 annual meeting of the Association of Humanistic Psychology). Association for Humanistic Psychology Newsletter, Special Edition, Fall 1981.

[69] http://content.time.com/time/magazine/article/0,9171,969312,00.html

[70] http://knowledgenuts.com/2013/11/03/the-difference-betweenpsychopaths-and-sociopaths/

[71] http://www.psychologytoday.com/blog/wickeddeeds/201401/how-tell-sociopath-psychopath

[72] (I)n the mental health field there is some consensus that psychopathy is more of an innate phenomenon whereas sociopathy, which has a similar clinical presentation to psychopathy, is more the result of environmental factors (poverty, exposure to violence, permissive or neglectful parenting, etc.). http://blogs.psychcentral.com/forensic-focus/2010/07/sociopathy-vspsychopathy/

[73] http://www.charismanews.com/opinion/the-flamingherald/43894-the-great-deception-in-the-american-church

[74] Trump, Donald J.; Schwartz, Tony. Trump: The Art of the Deal (Kindle Locations 821-822). Random House Publishing Group. Kindle Edition.

[75] Ibid. Kindle Locations 904-906.

[76] Ibid. p. 45.

[77] Ibid. p. 209.

[78] Ibid. p. 206.

[79] Steven Furtick, (Un)Qualified: How God Uses Broken People to Do Big Things, Colorado Springs, Colorado: Multnomah Books, 2016, p.8.

[80] Ibid.

[81] Jeremiah, David. God Loves You: He Always Has—He Always Will. New York, Boston, Nashville: Faith Words, 2012, p. xii.

[82] Ibid, p. 3.

[83] Yancey, Philip, What's So Amazing About Grace? Grand Rapids: Zondervan Publishing House, 1997, p. 45.

[84] Ibid., p. 15.

[85] Ibid., p. 70.

[86] Yancey, p. 71.

[87] Ibid., p. 72.

[88] Keller, Timothy. *The Freedom of Self Forgetfulness,* Publishing. Kindle Edition, Chorley, England, 2012, Kindle Locations 294-295..

[89] Ibid.

[90] Thayer, Joseph Henry, Greek-English Lexicon of the New Testament, Grand Rapids: Zondervan Publishing House, 1970, p. 549.

[91] Jeremiah, p. 21.

[92] Jeremiah, p. 19.

[93] Ibid., p. 272.

[94] http://www.christianitytoday.com/ct/2013/december-webonly/wolf-of-wall-street.html

[95] http://blogs.thegospelcoalition.org/trevinwax/2014/01/06/eva ngelicals -and-hollywood-muck/

[96] http://www.christianitytoday.com/ct/2014/january-webonly/why-we-review-r-rated-films.html

[97] http://blogs.thegospelcoalition.org/trevinwax/2014/01/29/chri stiansand-movies-are-we-contextualizing-or-compromising/

[98] http://www.desiringgod.org/articles/seven-questions-to-askbefore-you-watch-deadpool

[99] http://www.provenmen.org/press-releases/2014-pornographysurvey-of-christian-men-shocking-new-national-survey-reveals-highlevels-of-pornography-use-and-rampant-extramarital-affairs-amongchristian-men/

[100] http://www.christianpost.com/news/christian-sexpertsexpose-dangers-of-erotica-as-fifty-shades-tops-100-million-salesprepares-for-big-screen-115658/

Endnotes

[101] http://www.afajournal.org/2012/December/1212heroes.html

[102] http://www.booksandculture.com/articles/2005/janfeb/3.8.ht ml?pagi ng=off

[103] Tim Stafford, "The Third Coming of George Barna," Christianity Today, August 8, 2002, p. 34.

[104] https://wdtprs.com/2019/12/studies-when-highly-developedcultures-undergo-sexual-revolution-and-license-they-collapse-withmonotonous-regularity-within-three-generations/

[105] https://stream.org/ban-porn-a-qa/

[106] Boom, Corrie Ten; Elizabeth Sherrill; John Sherrill. The Hiding Place (p. 151). Baker Publishing Group. Kindle Edition.

[107] Ibid., p. 152.

[108] Marshall, Kirk and Hunter Madsen. After the Ball – How America will conquer its fear and hatred of Gays in the 90s. New York: Penguin Books, 1989.

[109] http://www.massresistance.org/docs/issues/gay_strategies/aft er_the_ ball.html

[110] https://www.barna.com/research/notional-christians-bigelection-story-2016/

[111] https://www.dailywire.com/news/courrielche-conservatives-next-frontier-patrick-courrielche

[112] https://psmag.com/news/the-miracle-of-trump-why-didevangelicals-deliver-the-votes-for-a-sinner.

[113] http://www.eyewitnesstohistory.com/titanic.htm

[114] http://www.sshsa.org/media/splash/SavingtheTitanic.pdf

Printed in Great Britain
by Amazon